Lochner v. New York

LANDMARK LAW CASES

&

AMERICAN SOCIETY

Peter Charles Hoffer
N. E. H. Hull
Series Editors

Titles in the series:
The Bakke *Case*, Howard Ball
Reconstruction and Black Suffrage, Robert M. Goldman
Flag Burning and Free Speech, Robert Justin Goldstein
The Salem Witchcraft Trials, Peter Charles Hoffer
The Reconstruction Justice of Salmon P. Chase, Harold M. Hyman
The Struggle for Student Rights, John W. Johnson
Lochner v. New York, Paul Kens
Religious Freedom and Indian Rights, Carolyn N. Long
Marbury v. Madison, William E. Nelson
The Pullman Case, David Ray Papke
When the Nazis Came to Skokie, Philippa Strum
Affirmative Action on Trial, Melvin I. Urofsky
Lethal Judgments, Melvin I. Urofsky

PAUL KENS

Lochner v.
New York

Economic Regulation on Trial

UNIVERSITY PRESS OF KANSAS

Published by the University Press of Kansas (Lawrence, Kansas 66049), which was organized by the Kansas Board of Regents and is operated and funded by Emporia State University, Fort Hays State University, Kansas State University, Pittsburg State University, the University of Kansas, and Wichita State University

Library of Congress Cataloging-in-Publication Data

Kens, Paul.

Lochner v. New York : economic regulation on trial / Paul Kens.

p.   cm. — (Landmark law cases & American society)

Includes bibliographical references and index.

ISBN 0-7006-0918-0 (cloth) : alk. paper). — ISBN 0-7006-0919-9

(pbk. : alk. paper)

1. Lochner, Joseph—Trials, litigation, etc.   2. New York (State)—

Trial, litigation, etc.   3. Bakers and bakeries—Law and

legislation—New York (State)—History.   4. Hours of labor—Law and

legislation—New York (State)—History.   5. Liberty of contract—New

York (State)—History.   I. Title.   II. Series.

KF228.L63K463   1998

344.74701'257—dc21   98-23809

CIP

British Library Cataloguing in Publication Data is available.

Printed in the United States of America

10 9 8 7 6 5 4 3

The paper used in this publication meets the minimum requirements of the American National Standard for Permanence of Paper for Printed Library Materials Z39.48-1984.

CONTENTS

EDITORS' PREFACE

From the moment that the decision of the United States Supreme Court in *Lochner v. New York* was announced, critics of the Court and its "freedom of contract" doctrine have pilloried the majority reasoning. In a famous dissent, Justice Oliver Wendell Holmes Jr. intoned that the United States Constitution did not incorporate the idea of social Darwinism. In later years scholars have called the "*Lochner* Era" a low point in the Court's history, for the case supposedly proved how out of touch the majority of the Court was with Progressive Era economic and social reform. For these critics, the doctrine of "freedom of contract" merely concealed or ignored the unequal bargaining power of employer and employee.

But as historian Paul Kens demonstrates here, the case raised other significant questions—of the impetus of state legislatures to enter the workplace and regulate hours, wages, and working conditions; of the role of courts as monitors of the constitutionality of state regulation of the economy; and of the place of economic and moral theories in judicial thinking. In *Lochner*, the Court tackled many of the complex questions that have since become the mainstay of our regulatory regime. But the outcome of the case—which we will not give away here—did not give any rule for the limits of state intrusion. Indeed, it only raised more serious questions about judicial legislative relations.

In his finely detailed, judicially balanced, and smoothly crafted narrative of the case and its times, Kens fits the legal history of the case into its economic and intellectual context. He begins with the actual conditions under which bakers and bakery owners labored. He takes his reader step by step through the passage of the New York State Bakeshop Act limiting the hours that a baker could work and then traces the progress of one small-bakeshop owner's suit against the state when it fined him for violating the statute.

All along the way, Kens allows the reader to see the larger picture—for example, the competing theories of free enterprise and regulation and the specters of organized labor and giant trusts that lurked at the edges of the case. But his special contribution is to sit the reader down at the benches in the Court to hear the arguments that the justices heard, then to whisk the reader behind the scenes to see the judges at work. Kens's clear and sound dissection of the reasoning of the majority opinions and the dissents peels away the various layers of jargon to expose the root differences of opinion beneath. Finally, Kens traces both the impact of the actual holding and the popular view of the case from the 1900s to the present.

Kens's work reminds us that once they are decided, cases like *Lochner* have two lives. First, they become precedent for later court decisions. As precedent *Lochner* had a checkered career, falling out of favor in the late 1930s, then being rediscovered by the Rehnquist Court. But cases like this have a second life, in legal scholarship. Over time, the academic lore of *Lochner* has become richer and more potent, and now it lies at the center of a dispute over the centrality of property rights in the Constitution.

ACKNOWLEDGMENTS

One advantage of revising a book is that it provides a second opportunity to thank the many people who have helped me along the way. My wife, Carla Underhill, not only provided encouragement but also took the time from her own busy medical practice to read and critique the many drafts of each chapter of the first version of this book. Long after she thought she was done with *Lochner*, I presented her with revisions for this paperback version. Wallace Mendelson and Lewis Gould were especially generous with their time and knowledge, providing direction and support from the earliest stages. Through questions, suggestions, and encouragement, they, along with Elspeth Rostow, Robert Clinton, and David Prindle, improved the work immeasurably. Thomas A. Green, John Brigham, and Kermit L. Hall also offered numerous helpful comments on the first manuscript.

Unlike some of the other great cases in American constitutional history, *Lochner v. New York* is not a case people outside of the legal profession usually remember today. Rather than lawyers and constitutional scholars, the readers I had in mind when I began this project were that larger group of people who are not aware of *Lochner* and its significance. I am extremely grateful to Peter Hoffer and N. E. H. Hull who, by creating this series, have made it possible for me to reach that audience. It has been a pleasure to work with the staff of the University Press of Kansas on this project, especially Editor-in-Chief Mike Briggs and Assistant Director Susan Schott.

Much of my work was done at the Tarlton Law Library, the Perry-Castañeda Library, and the Collections Depository Library at the University of Texas, Austin. I appreciate the assistance I received from the librarians at those institutions and others I visited.

CHAPTER I

Introduction

On April 19, 1905, the headlines of many of America's newspapers proudly reported that President Theodore Roosevelt had bagged a bear on his Colorado hunting trip. To many readers, the president must have depicted an ideal of the American way of life. The Rough Rider, hero of San Juan Hill, was a celebrity who radiated strength, self-sufficiency, and individuality.

If the readers had thought back about two years, they might have remembered another presidential hunting trip. It was during this earlier expedition to the woods of Mississippi that a famous symbol and more famous toy was born when the president refused to shoot a helpless bear cub. The toy and symbol was, of course, the teddy bear. It was inspired by a drawing of the event by political cartoonist Clifford Berryman, who thereafter used a little bear to depict Roosevelt himself. That such a simple event would become so newsworthy is somewhat surprising. Perhaps the president's act touched upon another American ideal. Mixed with the admiration of individualism and strength was a concern for the underprivileged, needy, and helpless, a distaste for unrestricted power, and a belief that everyone should have a fair chance.

On that same morning the more astute reader might have noticed reports and commentary on the United States Supreme Court decision in *Lochner v. New York*, which had been announced two days earlier. At first sight, this would not have seemed a very important case. The person most directly affected, Joseph Lochner, was far from being engaged in a struggle of life or death. The owner of a small bakery in Utica, New York, he had been fined fifty dollars for violating a state law known as the Bakeshop Act. This statute regulated the baking industry in two separate ways: by setting minimum standards for sanitation and by providing that bakeshop employees could not be worked more than ten hours a day or sixty hours a week. Lochner had been convicted of disobeying the second provision.

In contrast to the situation in the *Dred Scott* decision, which involved the issue of slavery, or *Brown v. Board of Education*, which dealt with school segregation, the outcome of the *Lochner* case would not itself be of paramount national importance. Nor would it be followed by civil war or rioting in the streets. But like these two, *Lochner v. New York* was to become one of the most controversial decisions in the history of the U.S. Supreme Court.

This case had touched a raw nerve connected to some very deep-seated ideas about the American political system, and conflicting ideals of the American way of life irritated that nerve further. It involved a question about the extent to which people could look to government to solve what they saw as the problems of their day. Were they to be left free to rise or fall on the basis of their own strength, or could government intervene to impose popular ideas of fairness? In addition, with its decision the Supreme Court intensified an ongoing argument about the extent to which the judiciary should be involved in answering such questions, and *Lochner v. New York* became a highly charged catchword in that debate. For more than eighty years it has served legal scholars as a poignant example of judicial activism.

What follows is the story of this case. But it is one that goes back further than the trial of Joseph Lochner and his eventual journey to the nation's highest court. To understand the significance of the case, it is also important to trace the march of political, social, and economic thought of the time and the circumstances that led to enactment of the New York bakeshop law. That is the objective of the first half of this book. As the tale runs from the 1870s to the third decade of the twentieth century, it touches upon urban baking industry conditions, tuberculosis and public health, sweatshops, tenement life, a variety of reform movements, the early life of organized labor, and New York politics, as well as developments in constitutional law.

Justice Rufus Peckham, who wrote the majority opinion in *Lochner*, justified the Court's decision to overrule the Bakeshop Act in part on the belief that the number of hours bakers worked bore no relationship to public health and safety. Responding, critics asked how the Court sitting in Washington could know anything about the working conditions in the bakeshops of New York City. Chapters 2 and 3 represent an effort to avoid the same mistake. The former provides a short sketch of the nineteenth-century baking industry and the environment in which those employed in the trade worked. Its goal is not only to determine whether bakers might have been justified in claiming that theirs was an unhealthy job, but also to determine the extent to which reform of the baking industry was motivated by concerns for health. This inquiry is continued in Chapter 3, which also deals with the history of American labor's efforts to secure a shorter workday. It covers the theoretical basis of the shorter-hours movement as well as its political successes and failures and seeks to determine the extent to which health and safety served as a rationale for limiting the workday.

In his majority opinion, Peckham argued that because it is not concerned with health and safety, the Bakeshop Act was merely a labor law pure and simple. His categorization raises a number of interesting questions. The political environment in late-nineteenth-century New York surely did not appear to be conducive to the enactment of such labor legislation. What accounts for the success in passing such a law? To what extent was it labor's victory, and who else was involved? Chapters 4 and 5 seek to answer these questions by providing an overview of the political scene and then following the progress of bakeshop reform from its inception to its successful enactment. It is important to appreciate that the *Lochner* case itself was only part of this longer-running conflict. Thus any attempt to explain it without first describing the political dispute from which it emerged would have all the drawbacks of a play that opens in the second act. Yet despite the importance of this case as a study in the role of the Supreme Court in the political process, little attention has previously been paid to the political and social background of New York's shorter-hours law for bakers.

The study of *Lochner* also involves the relationship between constitutional law and moral and economic philosophy. Oliver Wendell Holmes was one of many who criticized the decision as based on an economic theory that a majority of the country did not share. Holmes was speaking of the nineteenth-century concepts of laissez faire and social Darwinism. With his comments in mind, Chapter 6 explores the kinds of ideas about government, economics, and society that were in circulation from the 1890s through the early part of the twentieth century.

In addition to being a symbol of judicial activism, *Lochner* has provided law school texts with a standard illustration of the legal doctrines of liberty of contract and substantive due process. The latter is especially important because this interpretation of the due process clause of the Fourteenth Amendment provides the means by which courts have become involved in overseeing a wide variety of state-law-making activities. If for no other reason, the story of *Lochner* is important as a vehicle for explaining this significant aspect of constitutional law. Chapters 7 and 8 explain the evolution of these legal doctrines and their relationship to the moral and economic thinking of the day as they follow the progress of each side's case from the trial through the appeals process. Chapter 9 begins with the Supreme Court's opinion. In many Supreme Court cases, however, the decision seems to be best explained in dissenting opinions. *Lochner* is no exception. Justices Harlan and Holmes each authored hard-hitting, well-known dissents to the majority opinion. In these dissents, which are also the subject of the ninth chapter, the full implications of the *Lochner* case come to light, and the reasons for its lasting importance are discovered.

The *Lochner* story is an account of the politics and personalities during an interesting period of American history. Spanning the years 1890 to 1905, it has one foot in the Gilded Age and another in the Progressive Era. From this perspective, Chapter 10 describes the initial reaction to the case and attempts to determine why there was a reaction at all. To complete the story, however, it is necessary to go a little further. Chapter 11 summarizes the impact of the case from the time it was decided until it was overruled in 1937—the *Lochner* Era.

These last chapters, along with Chapter 12, also examine the *Lochner* legacy. As the symbol of a conservative judiciary's resistance to reform, the *Lochner* decision received a great amount of attention from 1910 through the early years of the New Deal. Recently it has begun to work its way back into scholarly writings. For many modern students of the Supreme Court, it serves as a prime example of misguided judicial conduct—that of basing opinions on political or economic policy rather than on moral principle. Similarly it exemplifies an old and erroneous conception of the Constitution that emphasized

{ *Lochner v. New York* }

the economic rather than the humanitarian in defining individual rights. In contrast to the traditional view of *Lochner*, some modern historians maintain that *Lochner* is not an instance of the Court attaching laissez-faire-social Darwinian theory to the Constitution. They maintain that the case reflects the Court's attachment to pre-Civil War ideals of Jacksonian democracy and free labor theory. The thrust of other recent scholarship is that the *Lochner* case was an aberration. These historians have pointed out that more regulatory statutes and labor laws were upheld than were overruled during the first thirty years of this century. Viewed in this light, they argue, the Court was not the laissez faire ogre it is conventionally made out to be. Yet another group of modern scholars challenges the conventional view by arguing that *Lochner* was correctly decided. Just as a theory similar to laissez faire has regained popularity in economic and political circles, so it has been growing in legal theory. For those writers who follow this trend, the Court's interpretation of the Constitution in the *Lochner* case represents something close to an ideal notion of liberty.

Following the Bakeshop Act from the birth of the shorter-hours philosophy, through the New York legislature, and on to the Supreme Court decision suggests, however, that *Lochner* did not represent an instance of the Court's enforcing economic policy rather than moral principle. Nor did it represent a clash between labor and the captains of industry. Rather, the conflict was one of competing ideals. The *Lochner* decision was, and remains, important because it signaled the Court's adoption of one of these competing ideals, laissez faire-social Darwinism, at a time when attachment to that philosophy was waning. There was an aspect of economic policy making in this choice, to be sure. In making it, the Court set a standard for testing the validity of reform legislation that lasted more than thirty years. But more important, as a matter of fundamental law, the Court had rejected the beliefs and goals of a large and influential group of mainstream Americans. These people were reformers, not radicals. Many were wealthy, many were professionals. Some had previously been attracted to the idea of laissez faire. An appreciation of the interests of these mainstream reformers, their participation in passing the Bakeshop Act, and their reaction to the *Lochner* decision goes far toward explaining why the case was not an aberration, why it eventually became so well known and controversial, and why it remains so today.

CHAPTER 2

Not Like Grandma Used to Bake

In the late nineteenth century, the baking industry was caught in the wave of industrialization and urbanization that swept through the United States. Industrialization drew former and potential home-makers away from the home and into the workforce, thereby increasing the demand for bakery products. Urbanization, at least to the extent that it was manifested in tenement-house living, had a similar effect. Ovens were not provided in all tenements. Even when one was supplied, however, life in these cramped dwellings, which were often shared by more than one family, could make home baking impossible. As a result, the number of wage earners in the baking industry went from fewer then seven thousand in 1850 to more than sixty thousand in 1900—a rate of increase almost twice that of manufacturing in general. Baking was a growth industry. Yet at the turn of the century almost three-quarters of the bread consumed in the United States was still baked at home.

At midcentury the American baking industry was just beginning to emerge. The mobile and rural society that existed before the Civil War had provided little opportunity for the industry to develop, and there were few large population centers in which it could thrive. There also was simply a strong preference for home-baked bread. Until as late as World War I home baking was a major factor affecting competition in the industry.

As the industry grew it actually developed into two separate branches. One, which became known as the cracker industry, supplied hardbread, crackers, and hardtack—nonperishable staples for use on ocean voyages and long overland trips. These were products well suited for mass production and wholesale distribution. There was nothing about this branch of the industry that would discourage combination and consolidation, and by 1880 regional "cracker trusts" began to develop. Competition among these large companies continued through the next decade. As late as 1893 the bakers' union reported that two of them, the American Biscuit Company and the United States Baking Company, were engaged in a fierce price war. But this war came to an end in 1898, when these companies, along with the New York Biscuit Company and the National Baking Company, merged to form the National Biscuit Company. With this merger one firm controlled 70 percent of the cracker industry. It was the type of monopoly that became the target of reformers' barbs and the symbol of the ills of the era.

Joseph Lochner and the other characters who played out the events culminating in his case were not part of the cracker industry. They were bakers of bread, and the conditions in this branch of the industry could not have been more different. The necessity of offering a fresh product, and the consequent need to deliver it quickly, discouraged consolidation into large firms. Although some local bakeries began expanding at the turn of the century, major trusts did not begin to form in the bread industry until after 1910. The first holding company did not exist until 1922. This company, created by William B. Ward, later merged with several others and became the target of a major antitrust suit in 1926. But between 1895 and 1905, the period during which the battles over the Bakeshop Act were fought, the supply of retail bread came from innumerable small businesses.

They were very small indeed. In 1899, 78 percent employed four or fewer people. The owners were called master bakers, or "boss bakers." Typically they were former journeyman workers who had broken away from their employers to form their own small bakeries. By taking that step, however, they were not transformed into captains of industry, nor did they even reach the status of a successful shopkeeper. At least in major urban areas, their lives more closely resembled those of jobbers in the tenement garment industry than those of shopkeepers or entrepreneurs.

It took little capital to set up a bakery shop. Unlike the cracker industry, which had become highly mechanized by that time, bread baking remained committed to laborious hand methods. There were, to be sure, some important mechanical inventions: the mechanical mixer in 1880, the molding machine in 1892, and in 1905 an invention for mechanically rounding and proofing the dough. New ideas were slow to be adopted, however. By 1899 only 10 percent of the bakeries used power machinery, and two decades later it was still found in only a bare majority of the industry.

Given that prospective master bakers did not have to worry about expensive machinery, all they had to do was get an oven and rent space to use it. But lacking machinery and methods of mass production, there was little that a normally prudent baker could do to improve efficiency. Meanwhile, other uncontrollable forces were working to limit profits. These small businesses had no control over the cost of their supplies, most of which were perishable. They could not negotiate the price of flour or yeast, nor could they build a stockpile when prices were low. On the other side of the scale, competition from home baking put a lid on their ability to raise prices. To make matters worse, any master baker who cared to look could see signs that predicted the end of their way of life. The experience of the cracker industry showed that the specter of mechanization and monopoly loomed. About the only variables over which boss bakers had any control were minor cost cutting, the wages they paid to their employees, and the terms and conditions of employment.

One of the costs that boss bakers could limit was rent, and they usually found the least expensive space in the cellars of the big city's ubiquitous tenements. Here was a location that commonly remained unused. It also supplied a floor sturdy enough to withstand the weight of heavy baking ovens. With their major demands thus satisfied, the vast majority of New York City bakers—about 87 percent of the industry as late as 1912—chose to locate their businesses in tenement-house cellars.

The problem, of course, was that these "ideal" locations were the basements of residential buildings, and dingy ones at that. If they were designed for anything at all, it definitely wasn't for commercial use. The cellar provided a passage under the house and was the location of the house drain. In the 1880s many of these sewers were made of brick and clay, and even the more modern ones of iron pipe smelled foul and often leaked. In cellar bakeries, sewers were often encased by wood and used for benches or racks. The floor, which was made of wood, dirt, or concrete, was usually damp or saturated. Walls were unfinished and ceilings were usually low. A state investigation of cellar bakeries in 1895 measured ceilings as high as 8 feet and as low as 5.5 feet.

Even the daytime light in these basement shops was inadequate. There were few openings to the outside, and those that did exist were often horizontal grates. Of course, this also resulted in poor ventilation. No breeze passed through to cool the shop, stifling in the summer or even in the winter when the oven was lit, and the grates failed to keep out the winter cold that chilled workers when the oven was down. Nor was there an outlet to dissipate the dust and fumes that were by-products of the baking process. Thus the turn-of-the-century bakeshop provides a stark contrast to the sterile stainless steel of a modern bakery, and it is quite unlikely that it bore even a faint resemblance to great-grandmother's kitchen. One thing that all of the reports and exposés of the baking industry agreed upon was that cellar bakeries were filthy and that the products that were turned out were a danger to the consuming public.

Causes other than the location itself added to this charge. The utensils, tools, and working surfaces used in cellar bakeries were seldom clean. Workers may have thought it hopeless to clean anything in their squalid environment, or they may have been ignorant, lazy, or fatigued; nevertheless they did not clean, and they were careless in handling the product. Reports describe the bakers themselves as being dirty. Washbasin and toilet facilities were usually inadequate, and workers seldom washed their hands before working with the food. One report observed that when moving heavy dough, bakers often carried it against their sweaty bare torsos and that knives used for slitting the loaves were carried in the bakers' mouths. The uncleanliness was aggravated in some shops, where boarding employees made their beds on workbenches, barrels, or sacks of flour.

Working in this environment could not have been very pleasant, but whether it could be considered dangerous, especially by the standards of the time, was another question. Bakers were exposed to flour dust, gas fumes, dampness, and extremes of hot and cold. They were not, however, exposed to work-related sudden death or catastrophic injury. Those who believed that baking was an unsafe job could base those claims only on the charge that these conditions increased the likelihood of disease.

Even then, if the standard for determining what constituted a dangerous trade was set at premature death, any claim that baking fell into that category stood on less than rock-solid ground. Although early statistics differed greatly, none placed the mortality rate among bakers especially high when compared with other jobs. It seems harsh, however, to require bakers to die in order to show that their work is unhealthy. There were other factors that may have carried that implication, but neither empirical research nor the study of disease was what it is today.

The major claim leveled by reformers was that the environment and work in bakeshops was conducive to the development of a disease called consumption. Modern medical dictionaries define consumption as an archaic word for tuberculosis, but the difference is more than one of name. Although tuberculosis is usually a disease of the lungs, it manifests itself in other ways as well. People suffering from nonpulmonary forms of tuberculosis in the nineteenth century would not have been considered consumptive. A more important difference, however, was that many wasting diseases and lung diseases other than tuberculosis were thought to be consumption. As a result of these uncertainties of diagnosis, much actual tuberculosis went unrecognized, while much of what was described as consumption in old medical writings was not really tuberculosis.

Consumption was to the nineteenth century what cancer is to the late twentieth. As the most feared killer disease of the time, it was given the monikers "captain of death" and "the white plague." The disease was highly romanticized: Keats died from it at an early age; others, such as Elizabeth Barrett Browning and Edgar Allen Poe, wrote about it. Alexander Dumas is said to have noted that "it was fashionable to suffer from the lungs; everybody was consumptive, poets especially; it was good form to spit blood after each emotion that was sensational, and to die before reaching the age of thirty."

Prevalent as this malady was, little was known about it. Reports of discoveries that would cure consumption were fairly common, but not as common as advertisements for curative potions. Typical was the testimonial for Duffy's Pure Malt Whiskey, which claimed to prevent and cure consumption and pneumonia, "the frightful ravages of these scourges which have so long baffled the skill of medical science." More "scientific" remedies ranged from prescribing inactivity to suggesting increased activity. They also included a wide variety of nutritional cures. Probably the prescription most commonly associated with consumption, however, was a change in climate. Even here, opinion varied widely about which climate to seek. Some advice suggested closing all windows and doors, but it was more common for doctors to prescribe time outside, either by the sea, in the mountains, or even in the desert.

It is not surprising that experts offered a wide array of cures. Until the late nineteenth century they did not even know if the onset of consumption was spontaneous, hereditary, or contagious. The disease was linked to habits and environment; fatigue, dusty air, sedentary life style, depression, tobacco chewing, and even the polka were among the things blamed. The high incidence of consumption among family members lent great weight to the theory that it was hereditary. Finally, in 1882, a German scientist named Robert Koch discovered the tubercle bacillus, proving that the disease most often described as consumption was bacterial and contagious.

Controversy and confusion did not end there, for Koch's findings were neither universally accepted nor widely known. In the United States, however, the commissioner of health of New York City was fairly quick to act. In 1899 he appointed Dr. Herman Briggs to do a study of tuberculosis. Briggs concluded that the disease was both contagious and preventable and offered a program that would, among other things, require reporting all occurrences of the disease. Despite the repeated efforts of Briggs and the health department to implement this program, it was not until 1907—two years after the *Lochner* case had been decided—that tuberculosis was declared communicable and that reporting its occurrence was required in New York City.

The tubercle bacillus was most commonly transferred from person to person on dust or dried sputum, and sometimes through adulterated food. Environment did not cause tuberculosis, but conditions affected the extent to which it was spread. At the turn of the century, living conditions and poor hygiene favored the disease. In fact, most people, especially urban dwellers, were exposed. Infection most often occurred during childhood, resulting in what is now called primary tuberculosis, a self-limiting form that often escaped detection. The more dangerous secondary, or adult, tuberculosis resulted either from reactivation of the latent original infection or from reinfection. In order to explain why the infection remained arrested in some people but resulted in serious disease leading to death in others, experts again turned to heredity and environment. As late as 1952, they argued that environmental factors such as overcrowded workshops, unsanitary living conditions, fatigue, physiological stress, and nutrition determined how the disease would run its course.

The nature of the disease tended to confuse statistics. The danger that bakeshop workers and reformers saw in cellar bakeries was not dramatic. They complained of the gradual undermining and "insidious dangers to health which resulted from doing this kind of work in cramped, airless, underground quarters." Tuberculosis, which modern medicine defines as "a chronic disease of long duration," clearly fits within this range of fears. Except for the so-called galloping consumption that killed Keats, tuberculosis, along with other respiratory diseases that might have been diagnosed as consumption, is not a quick killer. Rather these are debilitating diseases.

As the word itself implies, this sickness was characterized by a "wasting away." Malaise and fatigue were major symptoms; at advanced stages people were said to be able to walk only short distances without rest. They suffered from night sweats and lost weight. "Lunger," the slang term for a person suffering from consumption, was derived from its most dramatic symptoms. The impact of the disease on the lungs caused its victims to have fits of coughing and to spit up blood. Anyone who has observed the symptoms of more common respiratory ailments of our day, such as in a smoker suffering from emphysema, might well imagine that consumption could leave a trail of victims who plainly were unable to work but were not yet dead.

Journeyman bakers tended to be foreign-born males. The majority in New York were German. There were virtually no women or children in the trade, and most men tended to leave it at a relatively early age. Noting that there were few journeymen over the age of forty-five, a 1912 study speculated that after twenty or thirty years some became master bakers, whereas many others "get into such a debilitated condition physically that they are unfit for the trade and drift into some easier occupation." But sickness was probably not the only reason for their quitting. The day-to-day living of a baker in the nineteenth century provided many other incentives.

Baking was not an easy job. Journeymen began the process by

firing up the oven, usually with wood, coal, or coke. As the oven heated, they began sifting flour, preparing yeast, and kneading dough. These fatiguing processes were made harder by the quantity of materials used—these men were not working with cups and tablespoons. Flour, for example, came in barrels or sacks weighing between one hundred forty and two hundred pounds. It was sifted by being dumped into a trough and shoveled into a sifter.

Arduous though it was, the labor itself was not the primary source of the bakers' dissatisfaction with their circumstances. Wages in this trade were traditionally low. In 1894 few bakeshop employees made more than twelve dollars per week, and conventions of the trade watered down even this amount. At least until the turn of the century permanent employees were expected to board with the master baker, and the price of board was taken out of their pay. Day workers were often hired by the "vampire system," which required men to linger around saloons that served as unofficial employment bureaus. There they would spend money on drinks while waiting in the hope of being called to a job. Yet even wages, though always in dispute, did not seem to be the number-one complaint among bakers. That honor fell to the matter of long hours.

Bakers complained that their hours were so long that marriage and a normal family life were impossible. Considered along with the requirement of boarding, this may not have been an exaggeration. When New York bakers went on strike in 1881, one of their demands was for a 12-hour day. Given that their workweek was either six or seven days long, this meant that they were seeking an improved workweek of between 72 and 84 hours! By 1895 it was typical for bakers to work 74 hours per week, but many worked longer. A deputy factory inspector told the story of one bakeshop in which the men worked 15 hours, six days each week, and 24 hours on Thursdays, for a total of 114 hours each week.

Even longer workweeks, up to 126 hours, were reported at the time. To make matters worse, much of the work was done at night. Often beginning between eight in the evening and midnight, a baker's workday might end in the late morning or early afternoon. Such long hours had a bearing on their health and the fairness of their wages. But for the bakers and other workers of this era, the length of the workday was an independent issue affecting the quality of their life.

Such was the business of baking at the turn of the century. There was not a struggle pitting workers against a corporate giant. Monopoly and the monetary standard, the major issues of the period, affected bakers only indirectly. The story was not atypical of industry in general, however. It was a portrayal of appalling working conditions, slums, and poverty. The history of the New York Bakeshop Act is also a story of competing forces. It involves many opinions about what caused these problems and what, if anything, should be done to solve them. An account of these conflicts and ideas is what gives *Lochner v. New York* life, and it is essential for a complete understanding of the case. It begins with one of the first major issues in American labor history: the movement for shorter hours.

CHAPTER 3

A Long Struggle for Shorter Hours

They are familiar today, but in the nineteenth century not even the most visionary of labor leaders had yet thought of a minimum hourly wage or time and a half for overtime. Workers were hired by the week or, more commonly, by the day. Two dollars per day might be the agreement, the amount of pay bearing no relationship to the number of hours that the employee was expected to work during that day. There being no standard for what constituted a day's work, this could mean anything; more often than not it meant that the workday would exceed ten hours.

Some isolated examples of success in negotiating for shorter hours existed. Early in the century favored trades used their strong bargaining power to fix the length of the workday. One of the earliest success stories came out of Philadelphia, where journeyman millwrights and machinists were said to have met at a tavern and passed a resolution that "ten hours of labor were enough for one day." In most industrial jobs, however, the length of the workday was not ordinarily a negotiable item. Dawn to dusk had been the standard workday for farmers and artisans in preindustrial society, and the baking industry was only one of many in which employers sought to keep it that way.

For the individual laborer the issue of hours was probably a secondary concern to wages. Yet in the years following the Civil War, the shorter-hours movement became the focal point for labor's demands. The demand for an eight-hour day led to the formation of the first nationwide labor organization, the National Labor Union, in 1866. Eight-hour leagues, which appeared in several states, subsequently picked up the theme. Then it appeared in the early platforms of the Knights of Labor, the American Federation of Labor (AFL), and other organizations of the fledgling labor movement.

The eight-hour movement's attraction was that it offered the opportunity of success by means of governmental intervention. If workers did not have the economic power to win the eight-hour day through direct pressure on employers, their superior power at the polls might enable them to enlist the government to help them toward that end. The issue of wages presented far too complex a problem for this tactic. A "fair wage" would differ from place to place, industry to industry, and time to time. By contrast, the hours issue in its earliest form seemed exceedingly simple. All it required was a definition—what constituted a legal day's work?

The complaint of the bakeshop workers was typical. A workday of twelve or fourteen hours, six and often seven days a week, simply did not leave enough time for leisure. The people most affected were not artisans or farmers, who might choose to work late to finish a job. Some worked in mines, the building trades, or other exhausting jobs; but most were unskilled workers passing the day in monotonous toil, often working behind labor-saving machines. The number of hours they worked for their day's pay was for them a matter of fairness. Leisure joined wealth as one of the supposed benefits of progress, and most workers were dissatisfied with their share.

Although fairness was the underlying rationale of the eight-hour advocates, they dressed their argument with the attractive trappings of duty. In a democracy, they pointed out, members of the working class must be more than a source of labor. They must also be competent citizens, and working from sunrise to sunset was incompatible with the responsibilities of citizenship. Long hours left no time for necessary mental improvement and cultivation, especially given that the vast majority of industrial laborers began working as children. Furthermore, long workdays left even educated workers insufficient time to consider public questions or gather with others for discussion of the issues of the day.

Eight-hour advocates further claimed that employers also would receive benefits from having an intelligent and educated working class. Modern industry requires skillful workers, they argued, and the requisite skills could not be obtained in an atmosphere that allowed no time for leisure. They predicted that a shorter workday would produce better employees in another way as well. The last hours of the day were the least efficient because fatigue reduced the ability to concentrate, thus slowing the worker's pace and increasing

{ *Lochner v. New York* }

the likelihood of costly mistakes. On the basis of this observation, eight-hour proponents argued that reducing the length of the work-day would not substantially decrease output. Some even claimed that output might increase because employees would work harder and miss fewer days. This argument linked the physical well-being of the worker with the concept of leisure. A person who worked fourteen hours a day was too tired to read, too tired to be concerned with social issues, and too tired for a proper family life. But physical well-being in terms of danger to the workers' health and safety was not the dominant theme of the eight-hour movement.

Predictions of the benefits of leisure failed to sway most employ-ers. The testimony of one mill owner in hearings before the Massa-chusetts Bureau of Labor Statistics showed that some were obviously more impressed by stereotypes. "Of spinners as a class," he said, "I believe them to be a rowdy, drinking, unprincipled set, and any concession of time to them would only be wasted and rioted away." Other employers believed that not only would leisure be wasted, it would be harmful to the workers themselves. Keeping workers on the job saved them from their own vices and the vices of their class. "Licentiousness, gluttony, drunkenness, exposure, bad habitations, noisy and turbulent homes will wear men out in half the time that steady labor in the mills at usual hours of work will."

If leisure was the desire that drove the eight-hour movement, fear gave it an added push. What workers feared most was unemploy-ment, an irony of nineteenth-century economic life that some labor theorists referred to as "forced idleness." Leisure might enhance the workers' life immeasurably; unemployment, by contrast, was a very tangible disaster. The eight-hour advocates realized that some trends of unemployment were caused by cyclical booms and depressions in the economy, but they believed that much of the problem was chronic and that chronic unemployment was linked directly to mechaniza-tion. "Machinery is discharging laborers faster than new employ-ments are being provided," complained Ira Steward, "but machinery must not be stopped and tramps must not be increased." The only remedy, he said, was shortening the workday. One of Steward's fol-lowers meticulously but crudely calculated that the introduction of the eight-hour day would increase the number of people employed in Massachusetts alone by over one hundred thousand.

Begun as a practical response to chronic unemployment, this line of reasoning developed into a general economic theory. Ira Steward, a labor leader whose only formal education was as a machinist's apprentice, was the man most clearly associated with the theory's development. It was not highly polished, but in some ways it anticipated ideas that would be circulating among professional economists almost a century later.

By spreading jobs and wealth among more workers, Steward argued, shorter hours would enlarge and permanently sustain the market for manufactured goods. Those one hundred thousand additional employed workers would also be one hundred thousand more consumers of manufactured products. For Ira Steward, consumption was the economic basis of production, and the laborer was as important to one as to the other. Relying on this emphasis on consumption, Steward argued that the well-being of the working class did not depend on the prosperity of employers, as was taught by classical economics; rather, it was the opposite that was true. The well-being of employers depended on the capacity of the masses to consume. Shorter hours benefited all—"the worker by a steady job with fewer hours, and the owner by steadier markets and greater profits, due to undiminished purchasing power. Why not keep the entire work force on the payroll but work them less?"

The task of making an economic case against the eight-hour day was relatively easy. All that opponents had to do was call upon the study of economics as it was taught at the time. Limiting workers' hours through legislation would reduce profits and would ultimately drive out capital, it was said. Capital and investment created jobs, therefore the reduction of hours would actually increase unemployment. By insisting upon a standard workday, the eight-hour movement would in fact retard the progress of its own goals.

The problem of unemployment would take care of itself, eight-hour critics argued, if it was left to respond to the laws of economics. With mechanization, productivity would be increased, prices would go down, and demand would rise. More capital would consequently be invested and thus more jobs created. In this prosperous atmosphere, even the people who were put out of work by mechanization would find jobs. Increased demand would return some to their old jobs. For others, jobs in trades that made new machinery or in luxury and service trades would become available.

That was the theory, but profit was the motive that spurred employers to insist on long hours. It was only reasonable, for example, to believe that more worker-hours at the new machinery would help pay for the cost of capitalization; and most employers believed that production would suffer by a decrease in the length of the workday. The issues of discipline, responsibility, and control also played a part in their position. "It is for the master to do the thinking," said one opponent of shorter hours. It was the employers', not the workers', responsibility to determine what effort was necessary in order to accomplish the task at hand.

The employers' tendency, however, was to avoid such selfish arguments and rest their case on tradition. Eight-hour advocates were accustomed to hearing that "it would not comport with our notions of liberty, nor should we deem it wise, or even expedient, for any government to interfere with the sphere of individual effort or duty . . . by prescribing the terms or conditions by which they dispose of their own labor." Over time "freedom of contract" became the phrase that identified these notions of liberty. And even in its earliest forms, one characteristic of the argument was especially evident: it emphasized that it was the worker's liberty that was being infringed upon.

In response most eight-hour advocates argued that their opponents' insistence that the conditions of labor resulted from a contract between an employer and an employee was a sham. Even in legal theory a contract occurs only when the parties reach agreement by bargaining "at arm's length"—that is, to some extent each party possesses a similar amount of bargaining power. But now when a worker takes a job, eight-hour advocates claimed, the employer sets the terms. Testifying before the Massachusetts legislature, one advocate observed that "an empty stomach can make no contracts. The workers assent but they do not consent." From this some were able to conclude that without a legal limit on the length of the workday, employees simply delivered themselves into bondage for a day's wages. Throwing a drape of reality over an esteemed ideal could prove to be a difficult task, however, and few eight-hour advocates were inclined to take the challenge. Most relied instead on their practical claims.

By basing their opposition to shorter-hours legislation on the traditional notion of liberty, employers had found an effective debating point because it was true. Resistance to interference by the government in the daily lives of its citizens had been part of the Jacksonian concept of democracy, a favored theory not of the elite but of the common American. This notion had its limits, however. Lord Bryce, a contemporary British student of the American scene, noticed a gap between theory and practice. The sentimental foundation for laissez faire was extremely strong, he observed; but although Americans imagined themselves devoted to this theory of noninterference, they were not reluctant to extend the actions of the state to ever-widening fields.

Modern studies have demonstrated that the gap between the theory of economic laissez faire and its practice was significant in nineteenth-century America and that in the last third of the century, state interference in economic policy was common. Despite rules, many of which persisted from the Jacksonian era, that were designed to limit the output of state legislatures, they passed an increasing number of laws touching upon American social and economic life. Railroad regulation, factory inspections, bureaus of labor statistics, antitrust laws, and health regulations were among the most common economic reforms. The prevalence of this legislation led historian William R. Brock to conclude that "Americans had a unique capacity for living in one world of theory and another of practice."

The eight-hour movement was surprisingly successful in its efforts to pass legislation, but it soon saw results that could later be simply yet graphically described as "the futility of victory." The movement's first goal was to pass laws that would declare eight hours to be a legal workday, and by 1868 it had won seemingly impressive victories. By then six state—Illinois, Wisconsin, Missouri, Connecticut, New York, and Pennsylvania—had passed eight-hour statutes. In that year the U. S. Congress also enacted a statute that applied to federal employees.

The popularity of an eight-hour day had obviously given proponents a degree of political clout. But events following the passage of the Illinois statute demonstrated the limits of their strength. Passed in March 1867, the Illinois law provided that a legal day's work was to be eight hours for all nonagricultural labor *hired by the day* on or after May 1, 1867. As the effective date of the act drew near, however, seventy Chicago manufacturing firms agreed among themselves to institute the practice of paying workers by the hour. The conditions of employment would be the same—workers would receive the same wage and work the same hours. Nothing would change except the way in which employers said laborers were being paid.

Appalled by what they saw as an obvious subterfuge for evading the law, trade unions prepared to fight for its enforcement. Their first step was impressive: thousands of marchers took to the streets on May 1, 1867, to celebrate the effective date of the act. But although the next day some workers walked off the job after eight hours, most were required to return to their old schedules. This led to strikes in some industries, followed by riots, which eventually resulted in public opinion turning against the workers. Strikes continued for another month, but nothing approaching a general strike ever took place. Most workers continued at their old hours, marking a failure for the eight-hour movement.

The Chicago experience revealed one weakness of the shorter-hours movement: the workers' inability to follow through on their victories. But a more fundamental problem could be seen in the language of the laws that they succeeded in getting passed, for all of the earliest statutes contained a free-contract proviso. What this meant was that out of one side of its mouth the legislature said, "Eight hours shall constitute a legal workday," while out of the other side it whispered, "unless it is otherwise agreed." It was like crossing one's fingers when a promise is made. If the eight-hour advocates were correct in claiming that laborers had no bargaining power, the free-contract proviso made the promises of the eight-hour laws a dead letter.

The federal eight-hour statute followed the same general approach. Its language was purely declaratory, stating that "eight hours shall constitute a day's work for all laborers, workmen, and mechanics [employed] . . . by or on behalf of the government of The United States." Even this simple wording posed problems, however, because six years later the U.S. Supreme Court attached a free-contract proviso, ruling that the law was chiefly a directive by the government to its agencies and nothing in it prohibited contracting for longer hours.

The idea of creating an eight-hour workday for government workers and employees of government contractors was not confined to the federal jurisdiction. Several states also passed such laws. They were easier to defend than the general shorter-hours statutes because the government, also being the employer, was acting in a proprietary role. It regulated no one but itself. The hope of the eight-hour advocates was not only that the hours for a large number of jobs would be set at eight per day but also that the government would be setting an example that other employers would follow.

It turned out to be a bad example. From the beginning of the movement for shorter hours, confusion and disagreement existed about whether a reduction in the length of the workday would mean a concomitant reduction in wages. Those who favored the eight-hour day said, of course, that it would not, and they set out to convince the more skeptical. Workers are not paid for doing ten or fourteen hours of work, they said, they are paid the prevailing rate according to expectations. Throughout the movement's history proponents bolstered their argument by pointing out that in trades in which shorter hours were the norm, pay was also generally higher. For the less sophisticated this theme was put into a jingle:

> work by the piece
> or work by the day
> the shorter the hours
> the higher the pay

This theory was put to the test in a series of events concerning the federal law that involved two prominent New Yorkers: Roscoe Conkling and William M. Evarts. The former was a New York senator who, during the eight-hour bill debate in Congress, supported an amendment that would require federal employees' wages to be simultaneously reduced by one-fifth. That the amendment was defeated should have given a strong indication of congressional intent on the matter. Yet, acting on their own, some administrative officials reduced the wages of employees in their departments. Evarts, then attorney general of the United States, was asked to issue an official opinion. He responded with the vague statement that the law requires that "the same worth of labor shall be compensated at the same rate of wages it receives in private employment." The practice of reducing wages continued in some federal departments, and nothing more strikingly illustrates the problem of enforcing the eight-hour law than the fact that department heads even ignored two proclamations from President Grant ordering that the practice cease.

In the years that followed there were attempts to strengthen shorter-hours statutes by amendment. Some states added provisions that required that "extra compensation" be given to employees who worked longer than eight hours. Because the extra compensation was not defined, this addition did not have much effect. As late as 1918, confusion still existed over the exact meaning of the eight-hour day. The problem of reducing pay for government employees was addressed by "prevailing rate" provisions, which required that their wages be the same as those of workers who did the same jobs in the private sector.

Enforcement of the eight-hour day was also handicapped in a more direct way. Because there was no penalty for failure to comply with the early general laws, employers could simply ignore the directive. As the failure of these early statutes to achieve the goals of the movement became apparent, there was a trend toward attempting to write stronger language, but only in laws that applied to specific classes of workers.

Interestingly, many laws resulting from this second wave called for a ten-hour day. One author viewed this as a separate movement that focused upon exploitation of certain groups of workers and drew its strength from factory workers and philanthropists. Women and children were the primary objects of their sympathy, and the state of Massachusetts led the way in passing stronger laws for their protection. In 1874 it passed a statute that made it a misdemeanor, carrying a maximum fine of fifty dollars, to willfully employ women or children for more than ten hours per day.

Government workers were not as likely as women and children to receive a great deal of sympathy, but it was easy for the government to justify laws that regulated the terms of their employment. They were the second class of workers targeted for stronger laws. The federal act was amended in 1892 to make each violation subject to a penalty of one thousand dollars, six months in jail, or both. Many states eventually followed this lead by adding penalties to their shorter-hours laws. The impact of these penal provisions was destined to be watered down, however, by court decisions that narrowly defined the range of what constituted "government work."

This idea of targeting limited groups of workers in the hope of getting stronger legislation was next tried for adult men in specific trades. Once again sympathy may have been a factor for laws applying to hazardous industries. By the turn of the century several states had passed stronger legislation for the mining industry, railroads, smelters, and other obviously hazardous jobs. But it was actually industries that were not so clearly dangerous that led the way toward shorter workdays. Cotton-mill workers in South Carolina and Georgia had special legislation passed in the 1890s, and the brickyard workers and bakers of New York appear to have been among the first to succeed in having penalty provisions added. Even with the penalties, however, enforcement of the shorter-hours laws remained a problem.

———

To a great extent early labor unions had organized around the issue of the eight-hour workday. It was a matter, said historian Edward C. Kirkland, in which "the unions operated on the basis of a thought-out creed." A thought-out creed for justifying shorter hours may have existed, but the movement seemed naive about what it hoped to accomplish; it certainly was confused and divided about the methods that it thought would best accomplish it.

Although organized labor initially adopted the idea of seeking shorter hours through legislation, it eventually moved away from that position, favoring instead direct action or collective bargaining. This development may have been caused by organized labor's frustrating experiences with shorter-hours laws, or it may have simply reflected a change in its leadership. Samuel Gompers, who led the American Federation of Labor, was notorious in his opposition to the legislative method.

Gompers's opposition was to some extent developed from experience. Lobbying to secure legislation was costly and time consuming and never seemed to produce a law that was free from loopholes. When a law was finally passed, enforcement became the problem. Furthermore, success in the legislature was often overturned by court decisions. But Gompers's position also stemmed from personal predi-

{ *Lochner v. New York* }

lections. Organization added to labor's strength, he thought, whereas legislation tended to place the worker under the control of government bureaucrats. There was an additional element of self-interest in Gompers's position—there was always a danger that success in passing what he considered ineffective legislation would hinder the AFL's ability to organize.

Throughout the early history of the AFL there was strong opposition from within the organization over the leadership's decision to focus on organizing and striking rather than on getting legislation passed. Dissenters observed that direct action often required a strike, and the financial cost of taking that step would discourage many, especially the weaker unions, from seeking shorter hours. In addition, these critics noted that collective bargaining produced no benefits at all for the unorganized.

Elements who favored the legislative method had periods of success. During the AFL convention of 1894 they succeeded in passing a resolution that encouraged local affiliates to seek eight-hour laws in their home states, even though support for general shorter-hours laws had been conspicuously absent from President Gompers's address and the committee on resolutions had recommended against the resolution's adoption. Commenting on the 1913 Seattle convention, the *American Federationist* reported that state branches were once again urged to work for the enactment of general eight-hour laws.

The federation's standard position of seeking shorter hours by direct means was set fairly early, however. The conventions of 1884 and 1885 resolved that it would be in vain to expect the introduction of an eight-hour rule through legislation and urged unions to agitate in order to convince employers to restrict the workday. May 1, 1886, was set as a deadline, and a plan was developed for demonstrations and a general strike to take place on that date. This strike led to the infamous Haymarket riot that occurred in Chicago two days later. The incident began at a meeting organized by radicals to protest police intervention and the death of a striker. During the meeting an unknown person threw a bomb that killed several police officers. Negative public reaction to the riot resulted in the arrest and conviction of seven anarchists, who were charged with murder. Four were hanged, one committed suicide in jail, and the remaining two were later pardoned by Illinois governor John P. Altgeld.

Following the Haymarket debacle, the AFL assumed a low profile with respect to the drive for an eight-hour workday. It was not until 1890 that the federation resurfaced with a modified plan in which the eight-hour day was to be sought by collective bargaining on an organized union-by-union basis. Although individual unions continued to press for a shorter workday and the AFL continued to supply rhetoric for the cause, the 1890 plan was the central body's last full-scale effort to agitate for the eight-hour day.

New York's experience with shorter-hours legislation followed the usual pattern. Its first eight-hour law, which was passed in 1867, ruled that "eight hours of labor, between the rising and the setting of the sun, shall be deemed and held to be a legal day's work." Its language, which reads like a combination of legal jargon and the proclamation of a primitive chieftain, created no regulation or provision for enforcement. What is more, the statute included the free-contract proviso that "no person shall be prohibited from working as many hours extra work as he or she may see fit." A subsequent act in 1870 added the stipulation that extra compensation be paid for "overwork."

Government workers and those employed by government contractors were covered by a state statute passed in 1870. The potential for enforcing this law was improved by language that made it a regulation rather than a declaration and by the addition of a penalty. Public officials who violated the act were subject to a charge of malfeasance and could be removed from office. Private contractors would be guilty of a misdemeanor carrying a fine of one hundred to five hundred dollars. In addition, violation could result in their contract's being forfeited at the option of the state. A prevailing-wage provision was added to this law in 1894.

The idea of penal enforcement was carried over to an 1886 statute that made it illegal to employ "minors under eighteen years of age or any woman under twenty-one" for longer than sixty hours in one week. A person who "knowingly" did so was subject to a fine of between fifty and one hundred dollars, or thirty to sixty days in jail. This statute added a second innovation that favored enforcement: it authorized the appointment of two factory inspectors who were empowered to prosecute violations.

In that same year the first attempt was made at regulating working hours for adult men in a specific trade. Not what one would call a bold step, it forbade employing street and elevated railroad workers more than twelve hours in twenty-four and made violation a misdemeanor with no specified penalty. The trolley workers got an improvement with an 1892 amendment that made the penalty five hundred dollars. One year later businesses that were without question in the private sector were regulated by a statute that made it a misdemeanor to require brickyard employees to work more than ten hours per day.

This is the historical setting in which the New York Bakeshop Act was formulated. Although limited to a single trade, the act applied to all employees, including men. Its language was not merely declaratory; on the contrary, it set forth a clear regulation that "no employee shall be required, permitted, or suffered to work" in a bakery for more than ten hours in one day or sixty hours in one week. There was no free-contract proviso attached to the statute. Violation exposed the employer to the possibility of imprisonment or a fine that ranged from twenty-five dollars for the first offense to two hundred fifty for the third. Finally, borrowing the innovation from the 1886 statute that applied to minors, the act authorized the state factory inspector to hire four additional deputies to enforce it.

Although the workday ceiling of the Bakeshop Act was not pioneer legislation, it did represent the culmination of almost three decades of experimenting with methods and statutory language in the hope of producing enforceable and effective laws. It seems odd that such a major victory for the advocates of shorter hours was directed at this particular industry. It is even more curious that the legislation made it through the state legislature at all.

CHAPTER 4

The Politics of Business as Usual

When assemblyman Arthur Audett introduced the bakeshop bill before the New York legislature on February 12, 1895, he knew that the
opposition of one man in particular could be fatal to his proposal.
Although the Brooklyn Republican was serving only his freshman
year in the legislature, he must have been familiar enough with New
York politics to understand the power of Republican boss Thomas
Collier Platt. Based upon appearances alone, strangers would not
have guessed that Platt was the power behind the throne in New
York; they certainly would not have mistaken him for a Rasputin.
Photographs show a slightly built man with thinning hair and a
cropped white beard. His eyes, which one might expect to be burning
with the fiery conviction of a person possessed with power, look as if
they had been transplanted from a puppy that had just been caught
in the act. In an era that did not have thirty-second television spots
or telephone banks, it was customary for politicians to be good ora-
tors. Platt, however, was not. By most accounts he was a soft-spoken,
polite man. Unlike Roscoe Conkling, who was his mentor, or Theodore Roosevelt, who was often his tormentor, or many other political
figures of his time, Platt did not have a commanding presence. But
contemporaries agreed that Platt was in command.

Roosevelt observed that with the machine Republicans under his
domination, Platt was the absolute boss of the Republican party in
New York State. Others went even further. Platt ruled the state, said
Elihu Root, "for nigh on twenty years he ruled it. It was not the
legislature; it was not any elected officers; it was Mr. Platt. And the
capitol was not here; it was at 49 Broadway; with Mr. Platt and his
lieutenants." Given that Root, a distinguished lawyer, was speaking
in favor of state constitutional reform, one might be inclined to
think that he probably overstated his case. But his experience as an

insider in state and national politics lends weight to his comments; and many others, especially Platt's critics, corroborate him. Even Platt himself—with due modesty, of course—admitted to wielding influence in placing laws on the books of the state of New York.

Platt's most renowned place of operation was not his United States Express Company business office at 49 Broadway, but his New York City residence at the Fifth Avenue Hotel. It was there that he met with allies, advisers, and adversaries. And it was there that almost every Sunday he would join with his cronies in "Sunday school classes" to plan strategy. Most of the activity took place around two benches in a corridor of the hotel that was dubbed the "amen corner." There were differing versions of what went on. Platt described it as a place of sharing, where leaders of political, literary, and social thought were accustomed to exchanging their views. His account emphasized the famous people with whom he "swapped opinions in the corner." Presidents Lincoln, Grant, Hayes, Garfield, Arthur, Harrison, Mc-Kinley, and Roosevelt, along with governors, legislators, military officers, financiers, and even the king of England, were among those whom he recalled.

Critics viewed the amen corner as a place for scheming. *Harper's Weekly* called Platt "a wire puller chief," and the wire pulling for the legislative session of 1895, during which the Bakeshop Act was considered, was said to have begun with the choice of Hamilton Fish for the powerful post of speaker of the assembly. The speaker was officially elected by fellow members of the assembly, but the press assumed that Platt and his followers actually made the choice.

Interestingly, critics' version of the amen corner emphasized the role of more shadowy personalities. Fish was said to owe his nomination to Lou Payn, whose chief occupation was as a lobbyist at the state capitol. Payn was typical of many regular participants in the Sunday school sessions. They were not household names, but they were powerful in the Republican organization, often controlling their local parties.

The shadowy figures actually were present in the amen corner, and schemes undoubtedly were made. In February 1895, for example, the *New York Tribune* reported that the Sunday school members were unhappy with New York City mayor William Strong's political appointments. They had supported Strong in the previous year's election but did not think that they were receiving their share of his victory spoils. In retaliation they planned to kill or sidetrack any reform measures that he favored as they came up before the state legislature. And judging from the reformers' low ratings of the legislature at the end of the session, the Sunday school members succeeded in doing so.

In truth, however, the "corner" was probably the site of both sharing and scheming. Evidence that Platt was not above compromise can be found in his sometimes uneasy alliances with reformers such as William Strong, Seth Low, and Theodore Roosevelt and in his cooperation with men such as Elihu Root, Levi P. Morton, and Chauncey Depew, who were not members of his cadre. Critics of his leadership said that Platt actually led only where others wanted to follow. In fact, he seemed proud of his title "the easy boss" and claimed to have become leader by ascertaining public sentiment and getting abreast of it. But whether he was a boss in the fullest sense of the word or a conciliator or referee, Platt was the centerpiece of the amen corner. Both friend and foe agreed that in the 1890s that was the place where governors were made and state legislation was passed or killed.

Thomas Collier Platt was a lifelong Republican. In 1856 he wrote campaign jingles for the first Republican presidential candidate, John C. Fremont. Four years later he led torchlight parades in his county for Abraham Lincoln. Although he claimed to have "drifted into politics," Platt navigated a course that was steadily upward. By 1870 he had become the chair of his hometown Tioga County Republican Committee and was recognized as the local political power. In 1872 he was elected to Congress. About that time he aligned himself with U.S. senator Roscoe Conkling and a faction of the party called the Stalwarts. Under the guidance of Conkling, it became the dominant faction in New York State. Platt, who had become the consummate stalwart Stalwart, was soon elevated to the post of chair of the state committee, and in 1881 to the U.S. Senate.

His first term in the Senate may have set a standard of brevity. Having backed Ulysses Grant at the 1880 national convention, the Stalwarts were disappointed with the nomination of James A. Garfield for president. They were even more disappointed when, after they had joined the majority and worked for Garfield's victory in the general election, the new president ignored them when making federal appointments in New York. The patronage squabble that ensued ended with both Conkling and Platt resigning from the Senate in protest.

The two former senators hoped to be vindicated in a special election, but it turned into a more heated contest than they had expected. After more than a month of legislative balloting, Platt, claiming that he believed that he was hurting Conkling's chances, suddenly withdrew. His decision, it seems, had been as much a matter of tact as of tactics, however. A group of political opponents, who just happened to be standing on a stepladder and peering through an open transom into a local hotel room, had caught Platt in bed with a prostitute, and the story had leaked to the press. Both Platt and Conkling were eventually replaced by candidates of the rival "Half-breed" faction of the party. The defeat disheartened Conkling, who subsequently handed over leadership of the ailing Stalwart faction to Platt.

The Half-breeds controlled the state party until the late 1880s. In 1887 Platt's replacement in the U.S. Senate, Half-breed leader Warren Miller, came up for reelection. Before 1913 state legislatures chose U.S. senators, and in New York, as elsewhere, nominations were made in party caucuses. Platt and the Stalwarts put up Levi P. Morton to challenge Miller in the Republican caucus. A third candidate, Frank Hiscock, also entered the race. The first vote was forty-four for Miller, thirty-five for Morton, and twelve for Hiscock. The nomination was especially important to the Stalwarts, who believed that a defeat of Miller would break the Half-breeds' control over the party. But after numerous votes there was little change, and the danger became greater that Miller would be renominated. Platt proudly recalled that when stalemate became apparent, the Stalwarts astutely abandoned their second-place position and cast their lot with Hiscock. Hiscock, who was ever grateful for the Stalwart support, won the nomination. Thus, according to Platt, political savvy was responsible for returning Miller to private life and putting the Stalwarts in control of the party, with Platt at the helm.

The real coup de grace against Miller probably came about one year later, however, in a series of events that involved more chicanery than savvy. It began at the Republican National Convention of 1888, where, early in the balloting, Platt brought a sizable part of the New

York delegation over to support General Benjamin Harrison for president. Rumor was that Platt had been promised the post of secretary of the treasury if he threw his support behind Harrison. At the very least he would have had reason to believe that should Harrison win, he would express his gratitude by consulting with Platt in federal appointments affecting New York.

Harrison won the nomination, and the New York delegation's role resulted in Levi P. Morton being named his running mate. In what appeared to be an effort to unite New York Republicans for the general election, Platt agreed to the nomination of his old enemy Miller for governor. There was a strong suspicion in some quarters that this was anything but a peace offering. It was charged that Platt had concluded that Miller had no hope of winning a general election against powerful Democratic boss David B. Hill and that he helped to fulfill this prophecy by campaigning for the presidential ticket but not for Miller. "Harrison and Hill" clubs began to pop up throughout the state, giving some indication that this was in fact Platt's plan. His motive was that a Miller defeat, coupled with a Republican victory in the national election, would destroy any claim of effectiveness that the Half-breeds might still have. At the same time, Harrison's gratitude would result in federal patronage being funneled through Platt, causing lower-level party activists to look to him as their leader.

This plan was for the most part successful. The Republican presidential ticket won, and Miller was defeated in the gubernatorial race. Platt was not appointed secretary of treasury, however, and he was bitter about being overlooked; but under the Harrison administration he was given a good deal of influence over federal appointments in New York. This episode, according to one historian, marked the beginning of the reign of the "easy boss."

An interesting thing about the accounts of these intraparty battles is that virtually nothing was said about political policy or philosophy of government. Platt simply did not appear to have acted on the basis of political philosophy as such. The thread that tied his actions into a recognizable pattern was loyalty to his party, and more specifically to what he sometimes called the machine. "Early in life I became a believer in the Hamiltonian theory of politics," he recalled. "From that time I have held consistently to the doctrine of government by party, and rule of the party by the regular organization." The good of the state and the nation and the welfare of the party were in Platt's eyes one and the same.

This abiding concern for the well-being of his political organization was not without philosophical repercussions, for his idea of how to accomplish this was tied to the nineteenth-century political traditions under which Platt had developed. Historian Richard L. McCormick calls one element of this tradition distributive politics. Throughout the century, he explains, government excelled in distributing benefits to individuals and small groups for the purpose of promoting commerce and industry. Meanwhile it gave less attention to regulating, administrating, and planning for the enterprises it assisted. Harmony was the principle that guided distributive politics. The government gave rather than limited, a practice that at least until the turn of the century was not considered divisive. An individual might be favored or left out, but it did not set one group of interests against another. On a more theoretical plane it was claimed that the wealth produced from these government favors eventually spread itself out and that every element of society benefited from the general growth and prosperity that it fostered. It was an easy theory for politicians like Platt to believe.

The practice of distributive politics was reinforced by a symbiotic relationship that existed between the party machine and business. Businesses sought franchises, licenses, and other advantages from government; but they also sought protection from regulation and other state interference. The benefit to politicians and political machines came in a variety of forms. A common practice that helped cement the alliance between business and politicians found influential politicians and their relatives employed in high positions of private firms or their business handling lucrative contracts in industries that were particularly sensitive to government policy. Boss Platt was president of the United States Express Company, which did most of its business with railroad lines and the U.S. government. Others who were less well known but sufficiently powerful made the link as well. Edward Lauterbach and Lemuel Quigg, each at one time head of the New York county committee, had ties to rapid transit companies. Quigg, who was employed as a general adviser, admitted that his chief duty was to represent the company at the state legislature.

Perhaps the most famous link between business and government was provided by Chauncey Depew. His business connection was to the Vanderbilt family, whom he served first as a lawyer and later as president and chairman of the board of the New York Central Railway. His role was in large measure to look after their interests at the state legislature. Depew was not, strictly speaking, a part of Platt's organization. But as a leader of the New York Bar Association and as a U.S. senator, he was an active Republican spokesman.

Keeping in mind that Platt's main interest was for the well-being of his regular party organization, it is obvious that the most important benefit to be received from the symbotic relationship in this regard came in the form of campaign contributions. Republicans, of course, had no monopoly on business contributions—major businesses contributed to both parties in New York. Some years after the peak of his power Platt, testifying before a legislative investigation committee, admitted that the use of these contributions put candidates under a moral obligation not to attack the businesses that gave. But there was nothing unusual or illegal about the practice. The taint of insidiousness that attached itself to business contributions was caused by the large amounts of money involved and the increased likelihood that elected officials would be obliged to make immediate and direct returns. Efficiency, usually a laudable trait, darkened the taint still more when Boss Platt developed a system that funneled most business contributions through him.

The *New York World* described this system in a blistering editorial. It was an open secret in New York, said the *World*, that when the individual campaigns of Republican candidates had asked for contributions from "wealthy individuals connected with the great corporations," they had in many instances been refused. These individuals were willing to make contributions, the report continued, but said that "they would prefer to make payment to that well-known and trusted leader, Mr. Thomas C. Platt." Platt then distributed the money to individual campaigns by means of his own personal checks. In this way the boss was able to control the nomination of Republicans for the senate and the assembly. "The men nominated and elected by Platt money don the Platt collar," the report concluded. "The corporations which originally furnished the money communicate their wishes to the Boss, and the legislators do as their master tells them."

All this might be dismissed as the frantic sensationalism of an

opposition newspaper were it not for corroboration by more prominent and reliable sources. Theodore Roosevelt, for example, recalled
that the importance of business as an element of Platt's strength was
only imperfectly understood at the time: "Big businessmen contributed [directly to Platt] large sums of money, which enabled him to
keep his grip on the machine and secured for them the help of the
machine if they were threatened with adverse legislation." No questions were asked, and there was rarely any talk of specific favors. Platt
distributed the money in any manner that he saw fit. The result of
Platt's system, Roosevelt observed, was that "Republican bosses, who
were already very powerful, and in fairly close alliance with the priv-
ileged interest now found everything working to their advantage."

Patronage was another important element of nineteenth-century
political tradition; Platt learned its importance early and used it effectively throughout his career. In 1881 a Syracuse newspaper observed that during Governor Cornell's administration, it was Platt
who secured jobs for canal officials, prison wardens, county clerks,
superintendents of public works, and the like. "He puts men under
obligation to him and commands their friendship and services," it
complained. "Platt men are plenty in all the state departments at
Albany." Jobs were to be had in local government as well. Although
the Democratic machines got most of the patronage in New York's
big cities, Republicans could count on municipal and county jobs in
safe rural districts.

Federal jobs also were handed out—thousands of them in the cus
toms house, post office, navy yards, and other federal agencies located
in New York. Control of, or at least influence in, these appointments
was more important to Platt than his seat in the United States Senate,
and with good reason. Together these jobs and political plums generated the loyalty and motivation of thousands of party members.
And just as important a consideration for an aspiring political boss,
they were the source of power for those who were perceived as having control over their distribution. From the late 1880s to the turn of
the century, Platt was so perceived. In 1892 one prominent Republican estimated that twenty of the thirty-four members of the Republican
state committee were bound to Platt by personal and financial ties.
When confronted with this estimate Platt confidently responded, "The
Committee is mine if that is what you are asking."

There can be no doubt that along with these allies, Platt wielded substantial influence over the state legislature. His personal power, strong as it was, was further enhanced by legislative procedures of the time, which gave the speaker of the assembly, president pro tem of the senate, and several committee chairs a great deal of discretion over the progress of proposed legislation. Because there were no rules or methods that would force the leaders to advance a bill through the legislative process, each of them could kill any measure that came within the range of his authority simply by pocketing it. Passing favored legislation was more difficult; but they could put a great deal of pressure on free-spirited legislators by threatening to sidetrack the latter's proposals and legislative packages.

Hamilton Fish plainly owed his position as speaker of the house in 1895 to Platt. The president pro tem of the senate in that year, Edmund O'Connor, was also a Platt man. So loyal a follower was O'Connor that a New York newspaper complained that under his leadership senate business "was conducted chiefly by means of the long-distance telephone from the Capitol in Albany to the offices of the United States Express Company in New York."

The regular organization's control of the leadership of both houses of the legislature in 1895 was not merely a fortuitous coincidence—it was a fact of life in New York government after 1894. Theodore Roosevelt, who was elected governor in 1898, told an eye-opening story of Platt's asking him if there were any members of the assembly whom he would like to have appointed to a committee. Roosevelt replied that he was surprised by the offer because he knew that appointment of the committees was the prerogative of the speaker, and that the speaker— who was elected by a vote of the assembly—had not yet been chosen. "'Oh,' responded the senator [Platt], with a tolerant smile; 'He has not been chosen yet, but of course whomever we choose as Speaker will agree beforehand to make the appointments we wish.'"

Boss Platt undoubtedly viewed himself as a conservative in the sense of being sympathetic to business interests and opposed to the ideas of the era's reformers. Lauding Levi P. Morton as "the safest Governor New York ever had," Platt observed that "experience had taught him conservatism. He never was influenced by crazy theorists, but ran his administration as he did his great financial institutions." The Republican organization's conservatism was, however,

{ *Lochner v. New York* }

more a matter of self-preservation than of ideology. The traditional symbiosis made it unlikely that it would support legislative reform on matters of regulation, taxation, labor, or other issues that would adversely affect its business partners. With its provisions for regulation of the baking industry, inspection of bakeshops, and especially limitations on the hours constituting a workday, the Bakeshop Act of 1885 certainly seemed to fall into this objectionable category.

The history of Boss Platt's political organization hardly portrays representative democracy at its finest. But it is always tempting to get carried away with stories of unrestrained power and backroom deals. That the Bakeshop Act and even more important reform legislation existed indicates that the politics of New York at the time was not so simple or clear-cut. Although Platt undoubtedly had the power in 1895 to kill any piece of legislation and he displayed the ability to occasionally force through his favorite legislation against strong opposition, he remained part of a system that involved competition for public support.

One important characteristic of the political environment of that year was that the Republicans had not long been in control of the state government. In fact, as the 1880s came to a close, the Democrats seemed to be the ones establishing themselves as the dominant party in New York. The prior two decades had been marked by a stalemate: Republicans usually controlled both houses of the state legislature, whereas Democrats typically won the statewide offices. This pattern was partially explained by the makeup of typical voters who tended to identify with either of the parties.

Much Republican support in New York was rural, Protestant, and "old stock" American. This explained the GOP's success in controlling the legislature, because the apportionment of seats in that body heavily favored rural areas of the state. The rural counties also supplied Platt with an unwavering base of support. Of course there were Republican voters in urban areas. In New York City they tended to be concentrated in what were called silk-stocking districts. Like their rural counterparts, many of these supporters were old stock Americans, and most were prosperous members of the business, merchant, or professional class.

Republicans referred to their rivals as the party of rum, Romanism, and rebellion. Nationally the Democrats' strength was in the West and in the former Confederate states. In New York and the Northeast they were strongest in urban areas. Big city political machines, like Tammany Hall in New York City, relied heavily on new immigrants—"both living and dead, voting early and often." Irish Catholics formed the largest bloc of Democrats' secure votes, with the majority of Italians and other newer ethnic groups joining them. The Jewish and German communities were not so fixed in their support, however, and were thus an important swing vote in many elections.

As they entered the last decade of the nineteenth century, New York's Democrats had cause to be optimistic. Roswell P. Flower, their candidate for governor in 1891 won by a convincing margin. But this was not unusual; it was more significant that they had also gained control of both houses of the state assembly. It had required a sly political maneuver by Democratic leaders to gain three senate seats by contesting elections, but they had finally broken the Republican grip on the legislature. Following this "steal of the senate," the Democratic snowball continued to roll into 1892. With voters giving Grover Cleveland an impressive victory in the presidential contest that year and sending enough of his Democratic colleagues to Washington to make up majorities in both houses of Congress, talk of dynasty began to circulate.

Political prognosticators who talked of a Democratic dynasty were soon to be embarrassed, however, for within a few years the circumstances were dramatically and completely reversed. Republicans won all of the statewide offices that were contested in 1893, plus two special congressional elections. They also regained majorities in both houses of the state assembly. An important bonus came in the form of their election of a majority of delegates to an upcoming constitutional convention that had been called by the legislature while the Democrats were in power. In 1894 Republican gubernatorial candidate Levi P. Morton was elected by a substantial margin, and Republicans won most of the state and congressional elections. The Democrats' fate was sealed in 1896, when free-silver crusader William Jennings Bryan captured the party's presidential nomination but was soundly defeated by Republican William McKinley. The reversal that took place in these four years marked the beginning of a thirty-year period of Republican dominance both in New York and in the nation.

The most conspicuous explanation for the failure of the Democratic dynasty to materialize was the onset of a devastating economic depression. One of the worst since the Civil War, it began when the bankruptcy of the Philadelphia and Reading Railroad touched off the Panic of 1893. This set off a chain reaction of bank closings, more business failures, and declining prices that eventually brought farmers to their knees. By the end of the year the painful impact of the depression was beginning to be felt among the working class. In 1894 there were estimates of more than 4.5 million workers unemployed nationwide. That was 18.4 percent of the civilian workforce. It was a statistic of hard times comparable to the Great Depression of the 1930s, which at its worst point saw 24.9 percent of the nation's workers unable to find work. Bands of unemployed—the most famous being Coxey's Army—joined in dramatic though ineffectual marches on Washington.

When the economy collapsed, the Democrats had the dubious right to boast that they were in complete control of the nation's affairs. Undoubtedly some of the voter shift during the period could therefore be attributed to a knee-jerk reaction against the party in power at the onset of hard times. But some of the Democrats' problems were also of their own doing. As the party in power, they failed to develop an economic policy that would bolster public confidence. Adhering to a long-held policy of government noninterference and austerity, President Grover Cleveland's administration appeared to be doing nothing. The Democratic leader argued that the proper response to the depression was to tighten one's belt and wait for it to pass. It was a cold policy, displaying no sign of concern or sympathy for Americans who were caught in the economic mire. New York governor Roswell P. Flower took the same stance as he "reiterated the Jeffersonian faith that government governs best which governs least."

Republicans, on the other hand, had been pressing an economic policy that called for more governmental intervention. Based upon the idea that government had a positive duty to enhance the economic growth of the country, this policy did not espouse economic and social relief per se but rather a governmental role that subsidized and encouraged business. The vanguard of the policy was a protective tariff that, Republicans argued, would bring prosperity to business, farmers, and workers alike. President Cleveland was, quite to the contrary, a staunch opponent of protectionism. Early in the campaign of 1892 he had declared his intention to lower tariffs, and his administration's ill-timed initiatives to do so allowed Republicans to focus voter attention on economic problems.

The Democrats were the source of their own undoing in another way as well. Bryan's candidacy in 1896 revealed a party in turmoil. His single-issue campaign for the free coinage of silver satisfied many Democrats in the West and Midwest, but it repelled many of President Cleveland's former supporters in the Northeast. Bickering and fighting within the party were older than the 1896 campaign, however, and this divisiveness ran deeper than the issue of silver coinage. In New York it pitted several factions—supporters of David B. Hill, Tammany Hall, and Grover Cleveland's followers—in a battle over power, policy, patronage, and control of the party. This intraparty fighting, as much as anything else, resulted in the Democrats' losing what they had gained at the beginning of the decade.

Voter shifts during the depression and the Democrats' infighting each provided Boss Platt with tenable grounds to claim credit for victories in New York State. The political aftermath of the depression gave the regular organization an opportunity to claim that it had been instrumental in focusing attention on economic issues and convincing the voters of the validity of Republican policies. This strategy, the regular Republicans could say, had broken the traditional geographical, cultural, and ethnic bonds that linked voters to the Democratic party. The extent to which Republican gains could be attributed to factionalism among the Democrats testifies to the validity of Platt's belief in party unity and rule by the regular organization. He could hope to use that experience to silence critics and dissenters more effectively with a plea for unity and harmony. But of course critics were not silenced. One reason was that they knew that the regular Republicans were not the only participants in victories of the party. A new crop of reformers, noting the sizable Republican vote coming from urban districts, laid legitimate claim to a substantial amount of the credit.

Ironically, as Democrats were choking on economic issues and internal strife, the traditional base of their support was expanding. Beginning in the 1880s and continuing into the twentieth century the state's largest cities experienced a phenomenal rate of growth. In 1880 less than 40 percent of New York's population lived in cities of over one hundred thousand. Only twenty years later the number of urban dwellers had increased to almost 60 percent. Many of the new inhabitants had migrated from rural areas, but even more had come through the immigration center at Ellis Island. These immigrants, most of whom came from eastern or southern European nations, formed a pool of likely recruits for urban political machines.

With cities growing and immigration continuing, demographics seemed to be working against the Republicans. But New York's teeming urban environment—its living and housing conditions, working and social conditions, and even moral conditions—proved to be a perfect incubator for social reform movements. Settlement houses, tenement committees, and charity organizations flourished. At the same time, people who were concerned about the problems of city life turned their attention to its government. Accompanying social reform was a flurry of interest in civic reform.

Between 1890 and the early part of the twentieth century a variety of reformers, united in opposition to graft and corruption in city politics, organized continuous campaigns in municipal elections. This idea was not new. In 1871 reformers had formed the Committee of Seventy and organized a campaign that ended Boss Tweed's machine. In the 1890s however, civic reformers showed signs of renewed vigor and more lasting commitment.

The darling of the era's civic reformers was a man whom they nominated as their candidate for mayor three times. In social status, ideology, and education, Seth Low in many ways characterized the reform movement. Born in Brooklyn in 1850, he was from a prosperous family of merchants who could trace their roots on American soil back six generations to Puritan New England. The family, according to Low's biographer, had a tradition of social conscience and public service, and young Seth honored that tradition. He was a volunteer for the County Commission of Charities in 1878 and then a founder and president of the Brooklyn Bureau of Charities.

Low began his political activities by working for the election of

James A. Garfield and the Republican ticket in 1880. The next year he became a charter member of the Brooklyn Young Republican Club. Republican he was, but not the kind for whom Thomas Collier Platt much cared. From the beginning of his participation in party affairs he displayed the tendency to be a maverick. The primary interest of Low and his friends in the Brooklyn Young Republicans, for example, was to clean up local politics. The best way to do this, they argued, was to emphasize nonpartisanship in municipal elections. Low's nonpartisan stance was carried a step further in 1884, when he joined the ranks of the Mugwumps, Republicans who supported Democratic presidential candidate Grover Cleveland over their own party's candidate, James G. Blaine.

In 1881, at the age of thirty-one, Seth Low found himself in a position that was to become familiar to him over the course of the next two decades. His efforts in the movement for good government had placed his name on the tongues of many reformers as a candidate for mayor of Brooklyn. Low did not want the job, however, so their support soon turned to someone else. But Low possessed qualities that kept his name in the hat despite his resistance. His reputation was impeccable. Honest, intelligent, dedicated, and sincere, he was the perfect nonpolitician for a reform campaign.

Equally important was his political positioning: Low was fervent and unequivocal in his opposition to the machine of Brooklyn Democrat Hugh McLaughlin, yet it appeared that he would be acceptable to the regular Republicans. The spirit of guarded cooperation apparently ruled the day. With the backing of the reformers, Low became the nominee of the regular Republican organization. Breaking the Democratic stranglehold, Seth Low was elected mayor of Brooklyn in 1881 and again in 1883. During his two terms he was fairly successful in applying his ideals of nonpartisanship and businesslike city government. But the success of "good government" was not permanent. When Low declined to run again in 1885, the city returned to its old ways. A few years later Low became the president of Columbia College, but his political career was far from over.

When good-government forces began to gain momentum in New York City in the 1890s, much of the initial push was provided by a Presbyterian minister who was obsessed with cleaning up city government. Reverend Charles Parkhurst began his attack on Tammany

Hall in 1882 by using his Sunday sermons to denounce the "lying, perjured, rum soaked, and libidinous lot" who ruled city hall. Meanwhile, working through the Society for the Prevention of Crime, he began to gather evidence of the machine's wrongdoings. With the cooperation of the *New York Times*, the *Evening Post*, and other papers, incidents of illegal activities, payoffs, bribery, and corruption in the police department were widely publicized.

Here was more opportunity to malign the Democrats than Boss Platt could resist. Taking Parkhurst's lead, the Republican-controlled legislature created a committee to investigate the New York City machine. Hearings began in March 1894 under the direction of Senator Clarence Lexow. Conveniently timed, the Lexow Committee spent the remainder of the election year uncovering and publicizing sensational accounts of Tammany corruption. In 1894, with municipal elections in sight, independents formed a new Committee of Seventy to coordinate an attack on Tammany Hall. Although technically nonpartisan, the committee was composed mostly of nonmachine Republicans. It eventually settled on William L. Strong, a millionaire banker and former president of the Businessmen's Republican Club, as its candidate for mayor. The choice of an independent Republican turned out to be a good one, for it left the door open for an alliance with the regular Republican organization in what came to be called a fusion campaign.

The "fusion" of regular Republicans and urban independents assured that the ticket would be formidable. Indeed, on November 7, 1894, independent newspapers were hailing the victory. "Tammany Overwhelmed," shouted the headline of the *New York Tribune*. "New York State and New York City are redeemed from the thraldom of the worst set of political robbers and scoundrels who ever fastened themselves upon a civilized community." "Landslide in New York," it proclaimed. "Morton Beats Hill by 130,000 Votes—Republican Assembly Joins Republican Senate."

In the euphoria of the day following the election, independents envisioned a new era of reform under the leadership of Mayor Strong. The *Tribune*, edited by anti-Platt Republican Whitelaw Reid, heralded all of these victories with equal glee. With the passing of only two days, however, it became considerably more subdued about Republican victories in the legislature. Rejoicing turned to cautious optimism as it warned "We have, to be sure, a Republican Governor and a Republican Legislature. We ought to be able to count on the support of both for radical measures of reform . . . we do expect this. But we must not allow ourselves to become victims of overconfidence."

With victory less than one month old, a drawing on the cover of *Harper's Weekly* showed the alliance in a still darker light. It depicted a tiger—the symbol of Tammany Hall—lying placidly in a locked cage. Alongside was an open cage inscribed "next," and coming around it was a crowd carrying clubs and chains as they confronted Boss Platt. That the coalition that had elected Mayor William Strong, Governor Levi P. Morton, and a majority of the legislature was already showing signs of falling apart should not have been unexpected. To ardent independents the thought of being subservient to Platt was no more attractive than that of being Tammany's thrall. The Republican machine and the independents were very strange bedfellows indeed. For his part, Platt undoubtedly thought that joining in an anti-Tammany victory held the possibility of Republican gains in patronage and influence in the city. He also thought that he had an agreement with Strong that would assure just that, and was sorely disappointed when the new mayor failed to make good on his pledges.

Civic reform was an elixir that could give the regular Republicans an immediate inroad to the Democratic stronghold. It had potential side effects, however, and these presented serious and complex dangers to the health of Platt's organization. His was, after all, a political machine also. And although the immediate target of the independents was Tammany Hall, the fallout of their ideas—whether it be ballot reform, primary election reform, or civil service reform—was unlikely to be so specific. Even elements within the civic reform movement were destined to come into conflict. On the day following the election the *Tribune* predicted that the people's condemnation of Tammany had been so overwhelming that it was "shut out of the most remote hope of political resurrection." But Tammany boss Richard Crocker was not so impressed. Distinguishing his graft from the "dirty graft" that Reverend Parkhurst had found in the police department, he confided to reporter Lincoln Steffens that he had known all along that the voters would turn Tammany out. "Our people could not stand the rotten police corruption," he observed. Tammany will "be back next election; they can't stand reform either."

The German American Reform Union was one of the first and most important cogs in the reform camp to verify Crocker's prediction. Most German Americans, to whom beer drinking was part of their culture, were staunchly opposed to temperance laws—laws that, with the help of a bribe, were conveniently ignored under the Tammany system of government. Shortly after the election Mayor Strong appointed Theodore Roosevelt as the new police commissioner. Seeing it as his duty to clean up the department and viewing the idea of an officer accepting the hospitalities of the house as just another example of corruption, Roosevelt set out to strictly enforce the state's Sunday-closing laws. Within only a few months this new policy was beginning to show signs of its payoff. The German American Reform Union, frothing from the administration's avid enforcement of Sunday closing, voted overwhelmingly to endorse Tammany Hall's candidates in upcoming elections.

William L. Strong was not mayor of the New York City we know today. Old New York consisted of only Manhattan and part of the Bronx. Consolidation of this area with Brooklyn, Staten Island, Queens, and the remainder of the Bronx, which had been debated for years, was scheduled to take place on January I, 1898. The mayoral election was to take place in November 1897, and early in the year sides were beginning to form for the contest. The stakes would be high. One historian estimated that the new city would have an annual budget of $100 million and 35,000 employees, with an annual income of $40 million. The patronage controlled by the mayor of New York City, he observed, would be second only to that of the president of the United States.

The creation of a new reform organization, the Citizens' Union, was announced in February 1897. Although the leadership of this organization included many reformers who had participated in Mayor Strong's campaign, the Citizen's Union was imbued with a different spirit. The Committee of Seventy had been an ad hoc response to opportunity created by the Parkhurst and Lexow exposés. The Citizens' Union possessed a more long-range vision. Idealism, which grew out of a desire for clean government and belief in nonpartisan city elections, held the organization together as a participant in three mayoral elections. In 1897, however, idealism was to be its downfall.

It did not take long for the Citizens' Union to determine that Seth Low would be the perfect choice as the first mayor of Greater New York. Low, however, was reluctant to accept their nomination. First, he felt a strong responsibility to Columbia College and preferred to stay there. And second, although Low agreed with the idea that partisanship had no place in municipal elections, he also believed that fusion with the Republicans would be necessary in order to beat Tammany Hall and would have preferred to run on a "fusion ticket" similar to that of 1894. Nevertheless he accepted the Citizens' Union draft to head its campaign.

Many Republican party regulars supported fusion with the reformers, and Seth Low tried to bring it about. But Republicans eventually nominated a straight party ticket, with Benjamin Tracy, a law partner of Platt's son, as its mayoral candidate. Platt, the consummate party man, had decided that he would not throw his hat in with an organization that was so strongly dedicated to the idea of nonpartisanship. Some believed that he had learned from the experience with Mayor Strong that it would be easier to deal with a Democratic machine than with the independents.

Richard Crocker, Tammany's boss in absentia, also recognized the importance of the election. He had been commanding the organization from an English estate and returned to New York to personally take charge of the campaign. Quite confident of Tammany Hall's power, he tabbed the relatively unknown Judge Robert Van Wyck as the machine's candidate.

The Democrats were also split when supporters of William Jennings Bryan, using the banner of the Jeffersonian Democracy, placed Henry George in the race. George was not simply an alternative Democrat, however; he was a prominent reformer who had become internationally famous because of his book *Progress and Poverty*. His proposal was to solve the problem of poverty by placing a single tax on the unimproved value of land. George had also made a strong run as a labor candidate for mayor of New York City in 1886. Theoretically he would be an attractive candidate to the working class and would thus hurt Tammany's chances, but the true impact of his campaign would unfortunately remain unknown. On October 30, 1897, with the election only three days away, he died in his sleep. The Jeffersonian Democracy substituted his son and namesake, but Henry George Jr. polled only a small percentage of the vote.

Seth Low would eventually be elected mayor of New York City, but not in 1897. When the tally came in, Tammany Hall had regained control of the city. Low came in a distant second but demonstrated that the Citizens' Union could turn out a substantial number of votes. The Republican, Tracy, fell into third place. The combined vote of the Citizens' Union and the regular Republican ticket would have been enough for victory.

———

The mayoral elections of 1894 and 1897 provide a backdrop against which the various political forces in New York State at the end of the nineteenth century can be identified. They demonstrate that the relationships among them were not fixed. Regular Republicans and independents recognized that they needed each other, but they also disliked and distrusted each other. Even when they decided to join forces, each must have known that the union would be temporary. During those years each part would be jockeying to secure a share of popular support. Each group was, at the same time, trying to assure that its particular victory would not be lost through either compromise or the enactment of damaging laws.

The Bakeshop Act, passed in 1895, fell directly in the middle of this period. Like any other legislative proposal, it became part of the give and take of the legislative process. As the legislature began its work that year, however, only clairvoyant political observers were likely to have wagered that it would consider and pass a measure to limit workers' hours and regulate an industry. Independents were concerned primarily with election reform and general social reform; labor legislation was not part of their agenda. Conceptually it was the type of legislation that the regular Republicans would normally oppose. They were not intensely interested in every item of legislation that was proposed; but being in control of both houses of the legislature, they must have at least acquiesced to any bill that was passed.

What did the regulars hope to gain by supporting the bakeshop bill, or, perhaps the more germane, what did they think they might lose by opposing it? And who was pressing for its enactment? The answers to these questions will tell a great deal about how this minor item of legislation fit into a larger puzzle and what it represented in terms of the politics and thinking of the time. The place to start searching for these answers is in the 1895 session of the New York State Assembly.

CHAPTER 5

Tenement Reform Looks in the Cellar

When the bakeshop reform bill was introduced in the New York State Assembly in February 1895, bakers from New York City's East Side were on strike to demand shorter hours and better working conditions. Section 1 of the proposal, which set a ceiling for working hours at ten per day and sixty per week, and sections 7 and 8, which established penalties and provided enforcement, would accomplish just that. No doubt the bill reflected other goals as well. An important aspect of the law was regulation of the sanitary conditions of bakeshops, found in sections 2 through 6. There were minimum requirements for plumbing, floors, and the storage of products. Other provisions linked sanitation with improvement of the working environment. Washrooms and toilets were required to meet certain standards, as were employee sleeping quarters. The law's limitation on the hours of employment, however, was strictly a matter of improvement in the conditions of labor.

The timely strike in New York City served to dramatize that labor stood to gain most directly by enactment of this bill. It might be presumed therefore that organized labor would have been its most likely champion. But the strike also served as a reminder that many leaders of organized labor believed that collective bargaining was its best weapon. A large element of labor, especially in the American Federation of Labor, was less than enthusiastic about achieving the shorter workday through legislation. And even if it had been enthusiastic, 1895 was not the year to flex its political muscle. Just as the depression had hurt the Democrats, so it had been unkind to labor organizations. Not that the two were linked in any direct way—labor had problems of its own. It could not have expected much success in organizing unemployed workers to demand higher wages and shorter hours. This did not mean that unemployment made workers docile—

both the number and the violence of labor disputes were especially high in 1894. It was, for example, the year of the bloody Pullman Strike, in which labor was soundly defeated in both the streets and the courts of Chicago. Labor's image among workers and the general public was at a low ebb.

Organized labor did not have much political muscle to flex in any case. In fact, its first spurt of real growth did not occur until 1897, when membership was estimated at fewer than five hundred thousand. Thus in 1895 it was just entering puberty. On paper, labor's plan for dealing with the state legislature seemed that of a mature and well-organized body. Proposals were formally adopted at an annual convention. They were then assigned to a legislative committee that was also given the task of overseeing the progress of labor's platform. Various labor organizations were even officially committed to keeping a paid lobbyist at the state capitol. When it came to actual application of the plan, however, this appearance of organization proved to be deceiving. Labor simply did not have the ability to carry out its legislative operation as planned. Lobbyists were left to pursue their duties with virtually no money or resources. Until 1908, for example, the Workingmen's Federation did not even have an office in Albany.

Nor did labor lobbyists possess the standard tools, such as contacts, contributions, or favors, that other lobbyists could use to shore up their positions before the legislature. Like many of today's so-called public interest organizations, labor sat outside the center of the political power structure. It had little to give and little to take so far as most politicians were concerned. Although it could offer its endorsement to friends or threaten to blacklist unfriendly legislators, it was rarely able to deliver. These tactics therefore seldom produced the desired effect.

Labor's success hinged on its ability to convince politicians that it had influence over a sizable vote—an unenviable task indeed. Even after 1897, union workers made up only 5.5 percent of the workforce, and unions were unable to consistently deliver even these votes. Organized labor had to rely on the claim that it alone represented the interest of the working class, when it was actually one of many forces competing for working-class support. Although it usually depended on a bluff, labor's lobbying efforts were occasionally successful. Its claim was sometimes legitimated when its interest and the interest of the working class in general happened to coincide on a political issue. These instances of political agreement as well as sporadic victories in local elections enabled unions to display flashes of political strength.

The most impressive of labor's political efforts in the state was the New York City mayoral campaign of 1886, which came in the wake of several episodes of police brutality toward boycotters and strikers. Labor responded with an unusual display of solidarity. A wide variety of labor groups—from affiliates of the conservative American Federation of Labor to socialists—united to form the Independent Labor party and chose Henry George as their candidate. The election was a three-way race, and George received 31 percent of the vote. It was an impressive enough demonstration of strength to cause Henry George to declare that "never again would politicians look upon a labor movement with contempt." Indeed, in the year that followed his campaign a number of labor laws were enacted by the state legislature. But for all of this optimism, George's campaign must be kept in perspective. It was labor's best shot, and they lost. Abram S. Hewitt, the Democratic candidate, won the election. George followed not very closely behind, with the Republican candidate, Theodore Roosevelt, trailing in the distance.

It could be that Henry George was right. Politicians may not have viewed the labor movement with contempt, but neither did they hold it in high regard. Republicans, who got their money and support from big business and rural voters, rarely felt the need to placate labor unions. Realizing this, Democrats knew that they could usually appease labor by paying lip service to its demands.

To make matters worse, organized labor in New York was split into three parts. The Workingmen's Assembly, organized in 1865, was the oldest. The state affiliates of two national labor movements, the district assemblies of the Knights of Labor and the state branch of the American Federation of Labor, entered the picture a short time later. The three state organizations did give labor a presence in Albany, and there is no doubt that they sometimes cooperated. But they were also rivals, for both the ear of the legislators and the support of workers.

Rivalry exacerbated labor's problems in making itself heard in the legislature. If its hope for success depended upon cultivating the image of representing all workers, little was to be gained by having the same cry come from three different corners. Union affiliates and regional bodies, such as the Central Federated Union in New York City, added to the confusion. Many pursued their own legislative programs with little regard for the wishes of their state organization. Organized labor stood in the halls of the capitol building as a chorus of untrained voices without a director. Even government officials who might have been inclined to listen to their pleas were likely to be distracted by the cacophony that resulted. Commenting on the progress of his efforts, one labor lobbyist reported, "Members of the legislature tell us that if we could only make up our minds as to what we want we might get something."

Despite these handicaps, labor over the years did get something. A survey of the New York Bureau of Labor Statistics in 1895 showed fifty-one labor laws on the state statute books. Evidently labor was not powerless, but the significance of these laws can be overstated. They were exceptions rather than the rule, the result of periodic episodes rather than a strong long-term presence. Some may have been solely the products of labor's efforts; but many of the legislative victories in which labor participated, and for which it would have liked to take credit, were more likely the result of circumstances in which the interest of an otherwise weak organization converged with a timely issue.

Here is where an explanation of the enactment of the Bakeshop Act may be found. On its own, organized labor in New York was unlikely to have been able to guide the proposal through the 1895 legislative session, even if it had wanted to do so. A rush of popular support may have been what it took to induce labor to adopt the issue and to pursue it successfully. The question is, where did the rush come from? Before moving on to that question, there is another related factor to consider. George Groat put his finger on it when, in trying to describe labor's strength in 1905, he said, "Much depends on the individual ability of leaders, a force that cannot be measured numerically." Even if the opportunity for a political victory were to present itself, labor unions, which lacked money and full-time lobbyists, were unlikely to be able to take advantage of it without extraordinary effort on the part of an energetic leader.

In 1895 the Journeymen Bakers' and Confectioners' International Union of America had such a leader. His name was Henry Weismann. A native of Germany, Weismann came to the United States as a young adult. He had been a baker in the old country and, like many others, he left his homeland in search of a better life. For most who stayed in the trade this search yielded only long workdays at low wages in the small bakeries of American cities. But Weismann was more ambitious than most. His destiny did not lie in a tenement-house cellar.

When he first arrived in the United States Weismann settled in San Francisco, where he began his career as a labor organizer. In 1886 he became a leader of the Anti-Coolie League of California, an organization that he described as dedicated to restricting Chinese immigration. Primarily because of the enactment of the Chinese Exclusion Act of 1882, the organized anti-Chinese movement had already peaked by that time. Strong prejudice against Chinese workers continued to exist within organized labor, however, especially on the West Coast. If Weismann's recollection of the dates is correct, his anti-Chinese agitation was thus a little late, but it was not subdued. His enthusiasm landed him in jail for six months, convicted of possession of explosives.

The stint in jail was not a setback for his career, however. In the same year that Weismann joined the Anti-Coolie League, twenty-six bakers' unions from around the country held a convention and united under the impressive name of the Journeymen Bakers' and Confectioners' International Union of America. Soon after his release, Weismann was at work organizing bakers' unions in California. It was not long before he was asked to come to New York to serve as the editor of their weekly newspaper, the *Bakers' Journal*.

When he arrived in New York as the editor of the *Bakers' Journal*, Weismann must have impressed his new acquaintances as a bright, articulate young man. At the time, George Horn held the top position as general secretary of the international union; but no sooner did Weismann arrive than he began to influence the direction of the journal and of the union itself. In 1893 and 1894 he represented the bakers at the annual convention of the American Federation of Labor. By 1894 Weismann was for all intents and purposes acting as the union's public voice and leader. In a Labor Day article that year, a

New York newspaper erroneously identified him as "the international secretary of the bakers' union"—it was not until almost a year later that he officially assumed that post.

Henry Weismann never became a well-known figure in American history or even in labor history. Over a period of about thirty years he faded in and out of the limelight—always on the periphery, never a star. He did not leave a bountiful legacy. No biography or articles describing his activities are known to exist. But he did receive enough public attention during his life to enable later generations to get some idea of what he was like.

Weismann did not appear to be averse to taking credit, even where credit was not due. Nor was he bashful about promoting himself. The journal that he edited was replete with references to his own public comments, quotations from his own speeches, and excerpts from laudatory newspaper articles about him. Such opportunism and self-promotion, although not always considered to be admirable qualities, are traits that could be valuable to a floundering organization. By filling a void and taking the public point, Weismann might advance the interest of the bakers' union at the same time that he was advancing his own.

The bakers surely found in him a leader who was ambitious, energetic, and bold. Beyond that it is difficult to tell, from what he left behind, just how far his capabilities extended—whether he was extraordinarily intelligent or just average, cunning or bumbling, sophisticated or crude. He possessed one talent, however, that was essential and conspicuous in all of his public pursuits. More than anything else, Henry Weismann was a communicator. Articulate in writing both English and German, he was also a fluent and pleasing speaker with a slight German accent. But the skill of the greatest communicator would be of little use without a platform and an opportunity to display it. That opportunity was brewing for Weismann in a governmental investigation that started in 1894.

Early that year, following a series of newspaper articles that depicted the ugly life in New York City slums, the state legislature formed a special committee to study the tenement-house problem. This was not the first public inquiry into tenement conditions, and it would not be the last. The problem of housing the urban poor had given rise to a well-established reform movement. New Yorkers had been grappling with it since the 1830s, and the situation had gotten progressively worse as the city grew. The first study, launched in 1843, was undertaken by a private organization called the New York Association for Improving the Conditions of the Poor. Soon after that the state stepped into the picture, sponsoring several special committee investigations and passing some largely ineffective laws between the 1850s and the early twentieth century.

One of this series was the Tenement House Committee of 1894, commonly called the Gilder Committee after *Century Magazine* editor Richard Watson Gilder, who served as its chairman. Gilder was joined by seven other committee members. Two of them, Cyrus Edson and Edward Marshall, would play a role in the enactment of the bakeshop law one year later.

Edson, the son of a former mayor of New York City, became city health commissioner in 1893. A doctor, he had worked his way through the ranks of the health commission and was familiar with the variety of health problems common to an urban environment. His specialty, however, was an insidious hazard—adulterated foods. In 1886 he had written an article on milk adulterators who failed to take the precaution of removing snakes and toads picked up in the pond water they used, beverage manufacturers who used wells contaminated by city sewage, and candy made from sugar and a dangerous product called fusel oil.

In June 1895, about one month after the Bakeshop Act was passed, Edson resigned from the health commission after a disagreement with Mayor Strong and started a project for which he undoubtedly believed experience in public health had prepared him well. He spent two years working on a cure for consumption and finally developed a product called asepsin. Although sincere and conscientious, Edson was criticized for his work by some in the scientific community and was possibly cheated by a business associate. Asepsin turned out to be nothing more than a patent medicine, but Edson was not a huckster. The venture left him in serious financial trouble.

Edward Marshall was probably the least prominent member of the Gilder Committee, yet he more than the others deserved a seat on it. As Sunday editor of the *New York Press*, he had written the articles that led to the creation of the committee. Selected as its secretary, he became Gilder's right hand. In the months that followed, the two of them did most of the committee's work and developed a lasting friendship.

Marshall left the *Press* several years later and went to work for William Randolph Hearst's *New York Journal*. He was on the way to making a name for himself as a reporter when, in June 1898, his career was suddenly derailed. While working at the *Journal*, Marshall had become acquainted with Theodore Roosevelt. Having favorably covered Roosevelt's activities as police commissioner of New York City, he entered a cadre of reporters who circled around the future president. When Roosevelt was commissioned as a lieutenant colonel of the volunteer regiment for the Spanish-American War, he sent Marshall a "medal of the regiment" as a token of honorary membership.

Marshall accompanied the Rough Riders to Cuba during the summer of 1898 and was one of the reporters given the honor of joining the first troops to go to the front lines. At Las Guasimas, before Roosevelt's famous charge up San Juan Hill, a bullet from a Spanish gun shattered Marshall's spine, paralyzing him from the waist down. Eventually Marshall resumed writing. He wrote a history of the Rough Riders, several articles, and a couple of romance novels. He also continued to work at the *Journal*, but the injury must have taken a toll on his career as a reporter.

In 1894, however, Marshall was just beginning that career, and most of his energy was directed toward improving the conditions of urban slums. The Gilder Committee focused its attention upon three aspects of the tenement problem: the high incidence of disease and mortality resulting from structural defects and sanitary inadequacies; overcrowding of tenement houses and streets; and absence of parks and playgrounds in tenement neighborhoods. The first of these concerns caused the investigation to touch on the baking industry.

An analysis of fires in tenement districts revealed that a large number were caused by the operation of cellar bakeries. Much of the blame was placed on the "cruller fire," which occurred when fat, used in cooking fried pastry, was spilled. Although the committee's discovery of this problem was not what ultimately gave impetus to bakeshop reform, it did call attention to the industry. The committee's recommendations, however, were modest. They merely called for the enactment of specific requirements for fireproofing buildings in which baking was carried on.

A more extreme proposal would have been to license, regulate, or prohibit cellar bakeries, but Gilder was not prepared to go that far. Nor was he inclined to let the committee get deeply involved in the problems associated with tenement industries in general, even though some believed that the sweatshop system was an appropriate subject of the inquiry. On this point he and his friend Marshall disagreed. Marshall viewed the sweatshops as one of the major evils of slum life. They were most prominent in the clothing industry and employed mostly women and children, although sometimes entire families did piecework in their homes for incredibly low pay. He believed that the system added to tenement dwellers' misery by confining them to their already cramped quarters. Breaking from the committee on this matter, Marshall wrote a supplementary report that condemned the system.

Marshall was undoubtedly aware of the sweatshop problem before he began his service on the tenement-house committee. It was a highly publicized concern that many reformers wanted to see ended. Bakeries, by contrast, did not have so high a profile. The committee's study of fire hazards had introduced Marshall to this other aspect of tenement industries, and he set out to examine it in more detail.

On Sunday morning, September 30, 1894, the *Press* carried the result of Marshall's private investigation. "Bread and Filth Cooked Together," read the headline. What followed was a revealing account of the conditions in New York's cellar bakeries that must have caused some of that morning's readers to regret the first bites of their breakfast. Marshall relied on specific examples and graphic drawings to drive home the story: cockroaches on the walls and utensils; flour mixed in a tub that had just been used to wash a sick child's clothes; and a worker's filthy bedding spread upon flour barrels. If Marshall's own prose was not effective enough, he could sometimes count on a little help. One reader reported that he was skeptical about the article, but that when he broke open a roll and found a cockroach entombed therein he made up his mind that the statements might be facts.

The article was not a report of filthy environments and unhealthy baking processes alone, however. It also exposed the oppressive working conditions and "dreadful hours of labor" that were common in the business. Follow-up articles in the coming weeks would stress this aspect even more. It was the beginning of a new crusade for Marshall. His efforts in publicizing the tenement problem had resulted in creation of the Gilder Committee. Now he pointed his pen, loaded with whatever influence he may have gained in the past year's work, toward reforming the baking industry.

While Marshall was working on the Gilder Committee, Henry Weismann had been deeply involved with the American Federation of Labor. He was a delegate to the Denver convention of 1894 the year that Samuel Gompers was defeated for the only time in his long reign as the organization's leader. Weismann stayed in Gompers's camp throughout the convention. He also followed Gompers's line with respect to shorter-hours legislation, being opposed in principle to the idea of achieving labor's goals through the political process. Fortunately for the bakers of New York, however, Weismann was not one to handicap himself by being a slave to his principles.

Whether Weismann jumped on Marshall's bandwagon or whether he planted the idea of a bakeshop reform campaign in Marshall's head is impossible to tell. The two men obviously worked together even in the early stages of the publicity blitz. One week before the first (September 30) article in the *Press*, Weismann wrote a letter to the editor in which he called for a public investigation of the city's bakeshops. In a lead-in to that article he asked the *Press* to continue the good work it had done in exposing the terrible conditions of New York's tenement houses. He and the local union leaders also took part in Marshall's investigation and were the source of some of his data.

It was Marshall's influence, however, and the publicity generated by the *Press* that set the stage for success. Placing bakeshops in the glow of tenement reform tended to cast the issue as something more than a labor problem. It opened a door that allowed various established and prominent social reform groups to take up the cause. Tenement reformers, sweatshop reformers, and social settlement societies now could see in the baking industry the evils that they had detected in other facets of slum life.

Accounts in the *Bakers' Journal* give Henry Weismann much of the credit for orchestrating the activities that moved the bakeshop bill through the legislature. These were, of course, his own accounts and must be read with that in mind. Two things are certain, however—Weismann did not have the personal prestige nor did the journeyman bakers' union have the money or political power to pursue this issue successfully. If he actually did orchestrate the program, Weismann must be given credit for recognizing these two facts and quickly aligning himself with people who could make the difference.

One task that Weismann surely did have was to raise the level of enthusiasm in his own union and to line up labor support. He needed to keep the bakeshop issue alive among his fellow workers until the legislature met in January 1895. In October 1894 a committee of bakers presented a list of resolutions to the legislature, and in November a petition drive was started to encourage the legislature to take action. Weismann also published a pamphlet that detailed the bakers' complaints. These early resolutions called for improving sanitary conditions and giving the state factory commissioner charge of overseeing the industry. They did not mention limiting working hours, but the hours ceiling unquestionably became part of the proposal for bakeshop reform before the bill was introduced.

Arguing for the workday ceiling, Weismann echoed the rationale that eight-hour advocates had offered for decades. He reminded journeyman bakers that shorter hours would solve the problem of unemployment in the industry. "As soon as the 10-hour day and 60-hour workweek is a fact," he said, "the present number of idle men will decrease materially or disappear entirely." Just as it was for his predecessors, however, much of Weismann's argument was based upon an appeal to fairness. Bakeshop workers, he told the *Press*, worked such long hours that a normal family life was impossible. And when he finally got to celebrate enactment of the law, he reminded listeners that under prior conditions "the bakers had been robbed of daylight, robbed of everything that makes life sweet and desirable, and left to work almost incessantly, day and night."

Although it is difficult to tell just how much attention his journalistic campaign attracted, Weismann did have some small success in gathering labor support. The Central Labor Union of New York City, the cigar makers, garment makers, and possibly several local unions supported the bakers' bakeshop reform legislation. The state labor commissioner joined the cause early. Even the Socialist Labor party was recognized as a friend of the bill. Mention of the state branch of the American Federation of Labor or its legislative committee, however, was conspicuously absent from reports on the progress of the bill. Evidently the state organization did not carry the bakers' legislation, and it is unlikely that the Workingmen's Assembly or the Knights of Labor participated in any official capacity. To the extent that labor was involved in this effort, it was the journeyman bakers' own project.

The *New York Press* also claimed credit for the victory. Edward Marshall had promised to seek reform, and his participation on the tenement-house committee doubtlessly acquainted him with people who could help. He first enlisted the aid of Cyrus Edson, who, acting in his capacity as health commissioner, followed up Marshall's investigation with an official inspection of the city's bakeries. This provided both valuable data and the commissioner's personal influence during the campaign.

According to the *Press* thousands of letters urging adoption of the bakeshop bill were sent to the legislature, and the measure was supported by "many prominent persons interested in reform." The identity of all of these prominent supporters will probably never be known, but a few who are acknowledged provide a good idea of where the support came from. Edmond Kelly, a wealthy lawyer and founder of the City Club of New York, took up the bakers' cause, as did Felix Adler, a scholar and philanthropist and founder of the Society for Ethical Culture; the Reverend William S. Rainsford, pastor of the fashionable St. George's Episcopal Church; Father Thomas Ducey, rector of St. Leo's Roman Catholic Church; and General Frans Sigel, a Civil War hero and German-American patriarch.

Most of these people were attached to some established reform cause. Rainsford was active in the settlement-house movement, as was Adler, who also counted one of the early tenement-house committees (the Lexow Committee) and the Committee of Seventy on the list of his many activities. Kelly was a member of the prestigious City Reform Club and then a founder of the City Club and the Good Government clubs of New York City. Father Ducey, who had often taken up the workers' cause, joined the ranks of civic reform by urging Catholics to abandon Tammany Hall.

These reformers favored changes in the social system and government and were sympathetic to the hardships endured by the less fortunate, but they were not radicals who rushed along the outermost banks of society. Neither were they anarchists, nor socialists or communists, nor Molly Maguires. They were in fact mainstream Americans; if anything could describe them better, it would be that they were mainstream American elite.

Unlike some other members of their class, these men and women did not adhere to the theory of laissez faire and the individualism that it taught, nor did they fear cooperation with the working class. Felix Adler, for example, observed that "what [the philosophy of] individualism covers up with its doctrine of a hidden harmony following from enlightened self-interest is the fact that men are not equally able to protect their rights." It followed that government had a right to intervene in social and economic affairs in order to provide a functional balance between the rights of individuals and the needs of society. In 1894 Adler participated in the formation of the Social Reform Club of New York City. Dedicated to encouraging an exchange of views between "men of leisure" and the laboring class, the Social Reform Club supported labor unions in some of their political activities. Bakeshop reform was one of its earliest efforts.

A sense of sympathy and social justice provided one reason for supporting improvements in the conditions of the working class, but some mainstream reformers admitted to a slightly less altruistic motivation as well. Moderate reform, they believed, would tend to avoid an otherwise violent upheaval. Reform, in other words, was the way to preserve the existing social order. This point was made by Edmond Kelly, who warned that "the tremendous power of the workingman . . . awakening to his strength can no longer be overlooked by those who desire to see our present civilisation maintained." If educated and directed, he believed, that force would line up on the side of order. However, "if allowed to run riot in its war on capital, it would destroy the very foundation upon which our society is built."

The Reverend William Rainsford held a similar view. Although his church was commonly identified as J. P. Morgan's place of worship, Rainsford worked to make it a church for the poor as well as for the rich. He criticized religious leaders for turning their backs "on the bitter cry of oppressed and laboring people," observing that as a result they were powerless to help in the conflict between labor and capital. Although Rainsford recognized that the demands of labor could be as unjust as the demands of capital, this only served to emphasize the importance of God-fearing labor leaders as the country's bulwark against revolution. These thoughts were obviously on his mind when he wrote to the journeyman bakers, who were celebrating their victory. "I congratulate you on the moderation of your demands," he said, "and also on the moderate manner and wise methods which were used in presenting them."

In this way Edmond Kelly, William Rainsford, and the Social Reform Club were forerunners of organizations such as the National Civic Federation, which played an important role in initiating reforms during the early twentieth century. The National Civic Federation was created to encourage cooperation between the more conservative element of organized labor and a segment of the nation's business and financial elite. To many of the federation's members the influence of socialism among the working class and the worship of laissez faire by parts of the business community presented equally dangerous threats to the social order.

People who took up the cause of bakeshop reform had something else in common. Two years later most of them would be active participants in the Citizens' Union campaign to elect Seth Low as mayor of New York City. There is in fact reason to believe that Low himself actively supported the bakeshop bill. Low later declared himself to be opposed as a matter of principle to any industry being carried out in tenement houses. He was aware of the bakeshop problem, and he participated in some labor reform efforts prior to 1895.

Although leadership in civic reform came primarily from the city's elite, it was quickly recognized that long-term political success depended upon the ability to attract support from among the working-class population as well. In keeping with his philosophical ideals, Edmond Kelly was one of the most active in attempting to achieve this goal. Breaking from the City Reform Club in 1892, he founded a new club called the City Club of New York. The City Club, like its predecessor, was very much a social club composed of wealthy individuals. But Kelly came up with the idea of affiliating it with Good Government clubs, which would be located in each voting district and would include members from the working class. He thus hoped to form a bond between the wealth and influence of prominent reformers and the voting power of the working class.

Whether wearing the hat of civic reformers or of political independents, these people had practical political reasons for leading the charge for enactment of the bakeshop law. It was a perfect situation—the issue appealed to their social-reformer instincts, and participation was likely to earn them added respect from organized labor and the working class. The Seth Low campaign lends weight to this observation, even though it did not begin until a year after the bakeshop law was passed. Immediately after the campaign began, the Citizens' Union sought the backing of organized labor, counting several union leaders among its founders. Labor demands, including enforcement of the existing eight-hour laws, were placed on its initial platform. Even the choice of Seth Low, who had an attractive record on labor issues and was a labor arbitrator, was calculated to draw labor support.

It is also significant that Henry Weismann, who was by then general secretary of the bakers' union, joined the ranks of Seth Low supporters. Weismann's name was listed among the approximately three hundred people who formed the committee of organization of the Citizens' Union. Acting as an organizer of the mass meeting that kicked off the Low campaign, Weismann called for ratification of the Citizens' Union ticket. Thereafter he was active in the campaign as a member of the committee on labor and social reform. Working with this committee, he helped to write a pamphlet that tried to convince workers to abandon their loyalty to Tammany Hall, and he spoke in favor of the ticket at labor gatherings. Despite his claim that passage of the Bakeshop Act was accomplished with "no pledges and no political alliances," Weismann had clearly joined up with those whose efforts and influence had enabled him to claim victory for his union and for himself.

Bakeshop reform in 1895 was unquestionably a joint venture. A newspaper reporter supplied the opportunity and much of the drive. An element of organized labor participated, and a labor leader took on some of the responsibility for organization and direction. Finally, and probably most important, prominent and influential mainstream reformers provided the political clout.

The first step taken by the advocates of bakeshop reform did not foretell success. Neither sponsor of the bill was a political heavyweight. Arthur Audett, the bill's main sponsor, introduced it into the assembly. He was a former lithographer from Brooklyn, serving his first term in a short political career. Cornelius Parsons, who sponsored the bill in the senate, had substantially more political experience and prestige. A former lumber merchant, he had been mayor of Rochester and had served in the assembly before being elected to the state senate in 1891. Both were Republicans, but neither was part of the legislature's inner circle.

Nevertheless the proposal sailed smoothly through the legislative process. Introduced on February 12, it was assigned to the committee on public health, which soon sent it to the full assembly with a favorable recommendation. After the required number of readings, the assembly passed the measure on March 19 by a unanimous vote of 120 to 0. The bill's history in the upper house was virtually the same. On April 1 the senate passed the Bakeshop Act by a vote of 20 to 0, and it was sent to the governor for his signature.

The unanimous votes in both houses provide a sure indication that somewhere along the line the legislature's leadership endorsed the measure. There are any number of reasons why they may have decided to give their approval. The legislature's leaders were also leaders of the regular Republican organization and beholden to Boss Platt. The proposed law was unlikely to harm any of the organization's major contributors, but it might draw some support from the working class. It offered an additional bonus in that many of the workers affected were German Americans, and Platt was grappling with ways to keep that bloc of votes from rejoining the Democrats. A presidential election and state elections were coming up the next year, and the regulars wanted to do all that was possible to assure a Republican victory. As it turned out, Henry Weismann was among the labor leaders who supported Republican candidate William McKinley in 1896. What is more, the Republican leadership remained in an uneasy coalition with the New York City independents. The bakeshop bill offered one reform idea that posed no threat to Boss Platt's machine. Once it became a popular issue, there was no practical reason for the regular organization to oppose it.

It seems that by the end of the legislative session, everyone was

{ *Lochner v. New York* }

supporting bakeshop reform. Yet one disturbing question remains: That so many people either supported or voted for cleaning up and regulating the baking industry does not necessarily mean that they favored limiting workers' hours. This provision may have slid through the legislative process camouflaged in the other regulatory language of the bill. Although the placement of the hours limitation as the first section of the act weighs against that conclusion, this question might have lingered through history were it not for a bit of advice offered by Charles Z. Lincoln.

Lincoln, a lawyer from Little Valley in western New York State, was Governor Morton's private legal secretary and chairman of the statutory revision committee. Not a politician of long standing, he came into the limelight as a member of the Constitutional Convention of 1894. Joseph H. Choate, who was impressed with Lincoln's skill in framing the apportionment amendment that assured Republican domination in the legislature, was reported to have recommended his prestigious appointment.

One of Lincoln's duties was to review the bills that had been passed by the legislature and recommend to the governor what action he should take. When Lincoln received the bakeshop bill in early April, there was one provision that concerned him: he was worried that the limitation-of-hours provision of section 1 might be unconstitutional as it was written. At the time, the first words of the section read, "No *person* shall be required, permitted, or suffered to work in a biscuit, bread or cake bakery more than sixty hours in one week, or more than ten hours in one day" (emphasis added). Lincoln thought this language might prohibit bakeshop owners from working longer hours in their own businesses.

Lincoln conveyed his reservations to the bill's sponsor, Arthur Audett. On April 16 the two of them, joined by Edward Marshall, Henry Weismann, and "two of their friends from New York," met to discuss the matter. As a result of the meeting, the supporters of the bill and the governor's legal adviser agreed to retain the limitation-of-hours provision with one slight change—"employee" was substituted for "person" in the first line of section 1. Now the limitation on hours would not apply to individuals working in their own bakeries.

After the meeting, Assemblyman Audett took the necessary steps to allow the legislature to make the change suggested by the governor's counsel. The bill was called back for reconsideration by both houses. With attention now drawn specifically to the ten-hour provision, the assembly voted 90 to 0 and the senate voted 29 to 0 to pass the bill a second time. One hundred nineteen of New York's elected government officials could now be said to have approved the bill's limitation on workers' hours. On May 2, 1895, Governor Morton made the count 120, and the New York Bakeshop Act became law.

CHAPTER 6

Free to Bake or Left to Toil?

History provided the supporters of bakeshop reform with ample warning that their battle might not be over with enactment of the bill. States had been notoriously lax in enforcing factory or social reform legislation. Unusually strong enforcement provisions marked the bakeshop law as an improvement on past reform efforts, but their actual effect remained to be seen. Section 7 made the employment of a bakeshop worker for more than ten hours a day or sixty hours a week or the violation of any sanitary regulations of the act a misdemeanor. Penalties ranged from fifty dollars or ten days in jail for the first offense to two hundred fifty dollars and up to thirty days in jail for the third.

Criminal penalties were a major advance, but something more was needed to shift enforcement from an unreliable dependence upon employee complaints. This made the next section of the act even more important—it gave the state factory inspector authority to en force the law and authorized the appointment of four deputies to be hired for that purpose. In effect they could seek out violations of the law. Although four inspectors may not have been enough to cover the state effectively, this innovation could make the act potent. Without inspectors, enforcement would depend entirely upon the workers' willingness and courage to make complaints against their bosses.

Apparently drunk with success, the bakers' union thought that the 1896 session of the legislature would present a good opportunity to strengthen the act even more. They proposed amendments that would outlaw new cellar bakeries, protect employees who made complaints, prohibit domestic animals in bakeshops, and give the factory inspector minor additional powers. This time, however, the boss bakers were not caught napping. Led by Conrad Moll, they organized an opposition that was joined by tenement-house landlords and flour dealers. This group was not content to defend against new regulations. They counterattacked by proposing amendments to weaken the act, including a proposal to take away the four special deputy factory inspectors. Now rather than seeking improvements, the bakeshop reformers would have to fight to retain what they had won the previous year. The result was a stalemate. When the session ended, the substance of bakeshop reform remained essentially the same.

Changes in the law by legislative amendment did not represent the only potential threat to new reform statutes, however. Reformers often discovered that while they were relishing their victory in the legislature, it was being devoured in the courts. The history of eight-hour legislation had demonstrated how judicial interpretation of a word or phrase could water down the impact of a statute, sometimes even rendering it useless. But what was even more significant was the tendency to use the courts to challenge the very concept of reform. The most lucid example of that tendency occurred in New York in the tenement-house cigar makers' case of 1885.

Cigar making in New York City was an archetypical sweatshop industry. Workers were given the raw material to make cigars in their apartments, and they were paid on a piecework basis for the finished product. Industry conditions were bad enough that in 1883 and again in 1884 the legislature passed laws prohibiting the manufacture of cigars in tenement houses. The implicit purpose of the statute was to move the industry into factories where employees would work a fixed number of hours, at what one hoped would be a reasonable rate of pay, thereby relieving families of joining in the drudgery.

In May 1884 a cigar maker named Peter Jacobs was arrested for violating the law by making cigars in his tenement apartment. Jacobs had an unusual operation. In fact, if opponents of the prohibition had been allowed to write a scenario for a test case, they could not have done better than the facts that led to Jacobs's arrest. Unlike the vast majority of people in his line of work, who carried out their jobs in dirty one-room living quarters, this man occupied two rooms in a tenement house. He lived in one and manufactured cigars in the other.

Somehow Jacobs was able to secure for his defense the services of one of the most high-powered lawyers in the state. The lowly cigar maker would at the very least walk away from his troubles with the knowledge that he had something in common with a president of the United States. He and Andrew Johnson had both been clients of William M. Evarts, a former U.S. attorney general who was known as the prince of the American bar. With this support in his corner, Jacobs challenged the validity of the regulation in the state courts and won. The conceptual basis of Evarts's argument was that the statute violated cigar makers' personal freedom—that is, "the natural and inalienable right of property," which, he argued, "included the right to practice an honest trade inside the house." He observed that the industry "had simply discovered a method by which cigars could be manufactured by people in the bosom of their own families."

Perhaps Evarts often took his work home and was able to continue working while he enjoyed the company of his family and oversaw the environment in which his children developed. If he actually believed his own argument, this was how he envisioned the life of the tenement-house cigar maker. But the law's sponsor, Assemblyman Theodore Roosevelt, did not see quite the same image. Roosevelt was originally opposed to the idea of prohibiting tenement cigar making, but his opinion was changed by what he observed while visiting the tenement districts. He particularly remembered one room in which several children, three men, and two women worked making cigars. "The tobacco," he recalled, "was stowed about everywhere, alongside the foul bedding, and in a corner where there were scraps of food." The two families and one boarder in this room worked by day and far into the evening; they also slept and ate there.

These conditions mattered little to Evarts's case. The theory upon which it was based made them irrelevant. According to that theory there was a greater principle involved, which was best expressed by a quote that he used in one of his oral arguments: "The property which every man has in his own labor as it is the original foundation of all property, so it is the most sacred and inviolable. To hinder a poor man from employing his strength and dexterity in what manner he thinks proper is a manifest encroachment against the just liberty, both of the workman and of those who might be disposed to employ him." The authority that Evarts was calling upon then, and called upon repeatedly in oral arguments and briefs, was not derived from a legal source. He was not quoting the Constitution, a statute, or even the writings of the nation's founders. The source of his quote was the Scottish economist Adam Smith.

Smith's American successors, the laissez-faire economists, polished and advanced the principle that government should not interfere in economic matters. Their ideas dominated economic thinking from the early 1880s to the later part of the century, crossing
over into the political sphere as well. They were reinforced by the
growth of the philosophy of social Darwinism, and together they
created a legacy that formed a theoretical basis for opposition to
governmental regulation. It was a tradition that attracted a popular
following in the classroom and the boardroom and in the state-
house and the courthouse.

———

The American version of laissez-faire economics could be found in
the standard texts that were used prior to the 1880s. Reflecting classical British tradition, these texts defined economics as a science
based upon the systematic arrangement of immutable laws of nature.
The earliest laissez-faire theorists stated these laws in religious terms.
It was obvious upon the slightest reflection, proclaimed Francis
Wayland, "that the Creator has subjected the accumulated blessings
of this life to some determinant set of laws." This was not a surprising statement coming from Wayland, who was probably better known
as a theologian, but other economists held the same view. Arthur
Latham Perry, for example, stated that "the laws of exchange are
based on nothing less solid than the will of God."

As might be expected from a theory of economics, the most fundamental right to be derived from these laws was the right of property. The right of property, however, would be of limited value without the right to use it as one saw fit. Perry referred to this as the
right of free exchange, and he described it as the natural, self-evi-
dent, and inalienable right of all people to employ their own efforts
for the gratification of their own wants, either directly or through
exchange.

Private property and free exchange were not justified solely on
the basis of their status as natural rights, however. They were viewed
as the key to a system that, if allowed to operate uninhibited, would
bring general prosperity. That system began with and focused on the
individual. Its prime motivation was self-interest. The laissez-faire
theorists observed that each individual has different desires and dif-

ferent interests, and each will create a few products and need many. Therefore they must associate and exchange. But they believed that individuals will only exchange if it is in their own interest. The only motive for exchange, therefore, is the mutual benefit of the parties. From this the laissez-faire theorists concluded that in every exchange each party is richer than before—all are gainers. It did not matter whether this self-interest was based on enlightenment or greed. Guided by Adam Smith's invisible hand, the economy would function fairly and smoothly.

The economy would not merely function smoothly, however; reinforced by competition, it would grow and prosper. Machinery, inventions, and labor-saving devices would be developed. Individual skills would be utilized to the fullest. The amount and variety of products offered for exchange would increase. In short, the moral as well as the material welfare of society would be enhanced. So strong was this unwavering faith in the power of self-interest that it could even be found expressed biblically: "The Lord maketh the selfish man to work for the material welfare of his kind."

To laissez-faire theorists, the chief threat to the pursuit of individual self-interest and consequently the progress of society was economic legislation. Such interference was viewed as ineffective at best and in violation of the laws of nature at worst. This caused laissez-faire proponents to take an attitude toward the role of government that is sometimes referred to as the negative state. As the term implies, they envisioned a limited governmental role that primarily consisted of its maintaining law and order; government should do no more than make the rights of person and property as secure as possible. The struggle to so limit the government's role and attain the environment of free exchange was classified by Perry as one of the great struggles of history, equal to those for freedom of expression and freedom of opinion.

One of the staunchest advocates of the negative state was Edward Atkinson, who was neither an academician nor in the strictest sense an economist. An independently wealthy man with strong opinions and no hesitation in expressing them, he made his reputation as a popular speaker and a prolific writer of semipopular pamphlets, articles, and books on economic topics.

Atkinson's writings hammered out the consistent theme that

government should refrain from unnecessary interference with the freely chosen pursuits of the people and avoid attempting to reconstruct society by statute. Economic legislation, he claimed, was inefficient. Using his specialty, the cotton industry, as an example, he pointed out that economic regulation could lead to unemployment, that it made capital timid, and that it was the cause of such evils as intemperance, public corruption, and private fraud. He also charged that economic regulation was paternalistic. "If all workers were either ignorant or children, such legislation would be needed," he admitted, "but by the same logic government should also legislate what they eat, drink and wear, from whom they buy, and to whom they sell."

Another accusation laissez-faire theorists made against economic legislation was that taking economics out of the realm of natural law and placing it into the realm of politics tended to cause conflict between labor and capital. In the world of laissez-faire economics, the classes shared the same interest, and both Perry and Atkinson decried "the absurdity of the alleged conflict" between them. "This is no game of grab in which one wins and the other loses," said Perry. "It is a case of joint production, in which two parties conspire, and in which whatever helps to enlarge the gross amount produced, helps to increase the share falling to each party."

The only question that remained for laissez-faire theory was how to distribute the benefits of this joint effort, and for laissez-faire economists this was a matter of science. It was a science concerned only with pecuniary value; with respect to moral values it was said to be neutral. Although all laissez-faire economists agreed that labor was the source of pecuniary value, when speaking of the distribution of wealth in industrial society they actually began with capital. No matter how capital might be defined, the important point was that it created the demand for labor. It was said that the more capital that exists the stronger is the demand for labor and that therefore capital is the laborer's best friend. The value of labor, like any other commodity, was determined simply by the law of supply and demand.

Thanks in part to Malthus's theory that population would increase faster than the ability to feed it and to Ricardo's theory of diminishing returns from the land, economics at the beginning of the nineteenth century is sometimes referred to as the dismal science. But the American version was anything but gloomy. In fact, it was distinctly marked by a certain optimism. Edward Atkinson expressly rejected the theories of Malthus and Ricardo, claiming that they ignored the intellectual element in production, that is, human beings' ability to overcome the limitations of nature and to increase production by invention and organization. He may have been unusual among laissez-faire theorists in this respect, but the others were like him in projecting an optimistic view for the prospects of society as a whole. This view was enhanced by the tremendous advances in technological invention and efficiency that occurred after the Civil War. Progress elevated the moral status of capitalists because it was their wealth and skill that was seen as its cause. It also provided hope to laborers that they would share in the increased wealth. This hope was promoted to a prediction by Perry, who said that it was "a simple historical fact" that the percentage of earnings taken for profits would go down as the country became older and richer and that the cost of capital would decline as the amount of capital increased. On the basis of these facts, he concluded that the value of labor tends to constantly increase, "proving beyond a cavil that there is unwrought in the very nature of things a tendency toward equality of conditions among men."

If prospects for society as a whole seemed bright through the eyes of American laissez-faire economists, optimism for the prospects of the individual was even more evident. Individual success was, however, hinged to a recognizable set of moral rules. Value was said to be born of effort. Industry, frugality, and intelligence were the guidelines. Virtue and effort would be rewarded with capital and, presumably, wealth.

The end product might be aptly described as Calvinist optimism: the strong belief that every individual could succeed and that failure was simply the result of having failed to follow the Protestant ethic. Each individual's success was said to depend upon intelligence, aptitude, and devotion to an occupation. And although this may have seemed obvious when applied to people in business or professions, it applied to the laboring class as well. Courteous, skillful, steady, and contented workers were said to be the most attractive to employers. In order to be assured of satisfactory employment, each laborer had the responsibility to offer something unique in the way of excellence.

Given their belief in immutable laws of nature and the benevolence of the system thereby created, only two reactions to the problems created by industrialization were open to these laissez-faire theorists. One was to deny that progress and industrialization had in fact made life worse for anybody. In this, Edward Atkinson took the lead. Rejecting claims that the living conditions of workers had become worse in the industrial era, he pointed out that competition and invention had decreased the hours and drudgery of labor and increased the earnings of workers, both absolutely and relatively. If problems remained for the laboring class, they could easily be solved by developing the personal character and capacity of each member.

Atkinson took this idea to the limit. Observing that the working class spent most of its income on food, he theorized that much could be saved by educating cooks to be more efficient. Not content with talk, he invented an efficient cooking oven, the aladdin oven, and collaborated on a book dealing with the science of nutrition. Atkinson spent a great deal of effort and money trying to convince people that use of the aladdin oven would go far in alleviating poverty among the working class, claiming that it would be more effective than any of the schemes offered by "sentimentalist reformers."

The other reaction of laissez-faire theorists was to call for a stronger mix of the same potion. The cause of problems in industrialized society, they claimed, was not the market system itself but rather its impurity. Governmental interference with private property, free exchange, and liberty of contract were the pollutants. Efforts to solve economic problems through legislation, no matter how sincere, had the opposite effect. They upset the economic balance, destroyed the incentive for labor, and sapped the spirit of enterprise and the productive energies of the nation. Thus the laissez-faire solution rested primarily on economic grounds. Although not devoid of moral and social implications, it claimed to be above such considerations. If there was a need for an explicit moral and social justification of the negative state it would have to be filled by another source, and such a source was found in the teachings of social Darwinism.

———

Charles Darwin's *Origin of Species*, published in 1859, had an enormous effect on a wide range of human thinking. Reverberations are still felt today. In religion and education, for example, creationists attempt to overcome the general acceptance of Darwin's most basic findings and the teaching of his theory in schools. In fact, the broadest implications of Darwin's study are so well known that even most schoolchildren are familiar with the phrases "survival of the fittest" and "law of evolution." These concepts, or sometimes vulgar interpretations of them, are evident in almost every walk of life, from business and sports to biology and anthropology.

In the last half of the nineteenth century Darwin's ideas had a dramatic impact on philosophy and what was then the new field of sociology. The result was a school of thought called social Darwinism, and within it, specifically in the work of Herbert Spencer and William Graham Sumner, laissez-faire economists could find enthusiastic support for their views on competition, individualism, and the role of the state.

Referring to Herbert Spencer as a social Darwinist is somewhat of a misnomer because Spencer was actually working on his theory of societal evolution before Darwin's biological study became available. In fact, one historian credits Spencer with coining the phrase "survival of the fittest." Spencer, unlike his fellow Englishman Darwin, is seldom remembered today; but in nineteenth-century America he may have been even better known than Darwin. Richard Hofstadter observed that in the three decades after the Civil War it was impossible to be active in any field of intellectual work without mastering Spencer. But intellectuals were not the only ones who read Spencer. People in business, politics, and journalism, as well as the clergy, were familiar with his work.

Spencer's views on the role of the state can be found in his book *Social Statics*, which was initially published in Britain in 1851 and then in the United States in 1865. His philosophy differs from laissez-faire economics in its broad scope, which, as one historian noted with a bit of sarcasm, "offered a comprehensive world-view uniting under one generalization everything from protozoa to politics." The point is well taken, for in *Social Statics* Spencer was interested in more than economic justifications. He set out to develop a universal moral law.

Spencer observed that the difference between good and evil is simply a matter of the degree to which an organism is adapted to its conditions. From this observation he developed two general rules: (1) all evil results from nonadaptation to conditions; (2) where non-adaptation exists, it is continually being diminished by the changing of the organism to suit the conditions. Just as plants and animals adapt within their circumstances, the human race will adapt within the conditions of the social state. According to Spencer, humans needed one moral condition to be fit for the primitive state and another to be fit for the social state. The development of the race is a process of adaptation. Give individuals the ability to choose their own course and to seek to gratify their own desires, and evil will gradually die, while good will continue to develop.

These general rules led Spencer to a conclusion that he called the first principle. Referred to as the law of equal freedom, it held that there is only one limitation on individual freedom: one person's action may not interfere with another's possession of the same amount of freedom. In Spencer's words, "Every man may claim the fullest liberty to exercise his facilities compatible with the possession of like liberty of every other man." This, he said, is the primary law under which society must be organized.

The importance of the law of equal freedom to politics lies in the implication that it has for the role of the state, for Spencer believed that the state existed only to be the protector of the first principle. No desire to fulfill a secondary law, he said, can warrant breaking the first. If the state exceeded its role, it became an aggressor rather than a protector. It would be taking away the liberty it had been appointed to protect.

In Spencer's work it becomes evident how laissez faire and social Darwinism could be made to complement one another with respect to individualism and the role of the state. But this bond is even more evident in the work of William Graham Sumner, nineteenth-century America's most candid and incorrigible advocate of the laissez-faire-social Darwinian theme. Sumner has been described as a clergyman turned sociologist and pamphleteer, a description that more than anything else portrays his personality, frame of mind, and style. Sumner spent his early adulthood studying and teaching theology and even entered the clergy for a short time, but he rejected this vocation for more worldly studies. Eventually he became most influential as a teacher and writer of academic and semipopular books and articles.

During the last part of the century he held the chair of political and social science at Yale, where he was reputed to be one of its most inspirational and convincing teachers. If the fiery conviction that is characteristic of his writing is any indication, it is easy to see why.

Sumner considered himself to be above all a realist. Criticizing the idea of natural rights, he claimed that "our only right is to get out of nature whatever we can." Life and society were characterized by a struggle for existence, and morality in this struggle for existence was to Sumner a matter of balancing rights and duties. Duties were those virtues and activities that allowed people to survive and prosper; rights were simply the benefits that people were likely to receive.

Politics was not a matter of natural rights either. Sumner viewed political action as simply a refined form of arbitrary force, and he believed that rights were safe only when they were protected against its use. An immoral political system would be one in which one class assigned the rights to themselves while throwing the duties on others. This obviously would happen in a monarchy or an aristocracy, but he feared that the danger existed in a democracy as well. If a democracy was to be a moral political system, Sumner said, it must oppose claims for favor on the ground of poverty just as it would reject claims grounded upon rank or birth.

The implication for the state was that it should not interfere with the normal activities of people in their struggle for existence. When it did, somebody had to pay. Sumner cleverly labeled that person "the forgotten man," observing that "when . . . statesmen and social philosophers sit down to think about what the state can or ought to do, they really mean to decide what the forgotten man must do." Sumner's opinion of what they should do provides as candid a description of the negative state as can be imagined. "At bottom there are two chief things with which government has to deal," he said. "They are, the property of men and the honor of women. These it has to defend against crime."

To the extent that it was a moral philosophy, social Darwinism should have been broader than laissez faire. It should have accounted for the affairs of society in more than strictly economic terms. This may well have been the case, but both Sumner's and Spencer's brands of morality contained a stiff shot of materialism. They buttressed their laissez-faire conclusions with ideas of survival of the fittest and evolution, but both progress and fitness were measured in terms of material success. "The reason that man is not altogether a brute," explained Sumner, "is because he has learned to accumulate capital, to use capital to advance to a higher organization of society, and to win greater control over nature."

The concept of survival of the fittest offered both an explanation for poverty and a justification for inequality. In laissez-faire theory, poverty was either an unsavory by-product of overpopulation or a result of deviations from the system; but for both Spencer and Sumner it was simply a part of a purifying process. Spencer believed that the same rules that applied to the animal kingdom applied to humanity, and that these involved a stern discipline that was, in his words, "a little cruel so that it may be very kind." Turning the claims of humanitarians upside down, he said that they were "blind to the fact that under the natural order of things society is constantly excreting its unhealthy, imbecile, slow, vacillating, faithless members." People who failed to see this, he said, pursued a course that was injudicious and cruel. It only extended present misery and passed it on to future generations. Ultimately it hindered the development of society by encouraging propagation of the unfit and discouraging propagation of the competent. Sumner's view of survival of the fittest was similar, though somewhat more callous. The productive and conservative forces of society are wasted on the weak, he said; "they constantly neutralize and destroy the finest efforts of the wise and industrious, and are dead weight on the society in its struggle to realize any better things."

The social Darwinists' justification of inequality required only a minor extension of this line of reasoning, for "without inequality survival of the fittest could have no meaning." Within their framework, the only way to reduce inequality would be to take from the fit and give to the unfit. Not only would this neutralize the purpose of the laws of nature, it would also violate the social Darwinist concept of liberty. Sumner bluntly made this connection in an oft-quoted statement: "Let it be understood that we cannot go outside this alternative: Liberty, inequality, survival of the fittest; or not-liberty, equality, survival of the unfittest."

The social Darwinists' argument against reform by legislation took yet another form, one that has been labeled social determinism. Spencer held that society was passing through stages of development and that its course could not have been any different from what it had been. Continuing with the same idea, Sumner claimed that the fundamental mistake made by socialists and other reformers was that they assumed that humans had artificially organized society and that anything disagreeable could be changed by reorganization. They failed to understand that the social order had been fixed in accordance with the laws of nature. Sumner summed up the idea in a passage from an essay entitled "The Absurd Effort to Make the World Over": "Everyone is a child of his age and cannot get out of it. . . . The tide will not be changed by us."

This obviously did not mean that there could be no change. That would be inconsistent with the whole idea of evolution. What it did mean was that the state should create an atmosphere in which evolution could take place. This seemingly progressive position is revealed as conservative when one realizes that the proper atmosphere was created by the state staying out of the picture. Social Darwinism envisioned a gradual, natural change, unimpeded by any social scheme or design. "We need not resist change," said Sumner, "that is not conservatism. We may, however, be sure that the only possible good for society must come of evolution, not of revolution."

———

Gradual change was not the only characteristic that distinguished evolution from revolution. In order to meet Sumner's criteria for evolution, change had to be natural, which meant in the laissez-faire–social Darwinian tradition that it resulted from individualism and competition. The greatest contradiction to such natural change, the bane of proper development of society according to these theories, lies in the teachings of socialism. And adherents of the negative state found it practical to point to the danger of socialist ideas in order to lend immediacy to their cause.

The idea of natural change envisioned by Sumner was in fact challenged by a variety of nineteenth-century radical movements. Not all of them were socialist, however. The single-tax movement that sprang from Henry George's *Progress and Poverty* is an example. George suggested a radical restructuring of capitalist society by means of a tax on the value of unimproved land; but because he remained attached to the principle of competition, his theory was rejected by the followers of laissez faire and socialism alike.

There is little question that laissez-faire theorists exaggerated the danger presented by socialism. Yet socialism was a reality in nineteenth-century America, even if it often seemed to play only the role of scapegoat. Upheavals such as the Pullman Strike of 1894 were commonly blamed on socialists or anarchists. In some instances such charges may have been justly made, for socialism did have a following in the United States. The leader of the Pullman Strike, Eugene Debs, later polled close to one million votes as the Socialist party candidate in each of two presidential elections. American socialism also had an indigenous theoretical basis that found expression in the writings of a variety of theorists.

A native utopian socialist tradition, which dated at least as far back as the 1820s, received a boost in popularity toward the end of the century from a novel entitled *Looking Backward*, by Edward Bellamy. In the early 1890s about one million copies were sold. Yet the effect that the book had on a substantial portion of its readers was even more important. Clubs devoted to realizing the type of society described in *Looking Backward* began to spring up, first in Massachusetts and then throughout the country. By 1890 about one hundred fifty of these Nationalist clubs had come into existence. Edward Bellamy, by all accounts a quiet and introverted man, was propelled into the leadership of a reform movement. Enthusiasm was short-lived, however—the Nationalist movement lasted for less than a decade. But the impact of Bellamy's novel, his critique of the economic system, and the introduction of collectivist ideas lingered.

The key to Bellamy's utopia lay in replacing the economic system of competition with one based upon cooperation. In the words of his fictional character Dr. Leete, an economic system based upon competition "seemed like sheer madness, a scene from bedlam." Producers did not work together for the maintenance of the community, he observed, but only for their own benefit, and any increase in the aggregate wealth was purely incidental. Producers deliberately entered a field of business with the intention of destroying those who had previously occupied it. Their dream was to gain absolute control of some necessity of life so that they might keep the public on the verge of starvation and always command famine prices. This inefficient, ad hoc system caused periodic gluts and crises, and it led to the idleness of both labor and capital. The result was a society that suffered from a common insecurity, and consequently hoarded their wealth, which led to greater disparity between rich and poor.

Bellamy's solution was nationalization of the means of production. In a spirit of economic democracy, people would simply do what they had done in the political arena more than a century earlier—they would take collective control. Without this step, he claimed, political democracy was meaningless. With it, all production would be for use rather than for profit; inefficiency, inequality, and want would be eliminated.

The danger of such a change is that it could result in a loss of individuality and, in a sense, loss of the liberty so cherished by Atkinson and Sumner. Bellamy was undoubtedly aware of this concern but believed that the type of individualism encouraged by the competitive system did not represent the best of human nature. It was "merely that form of society which was founded on the pseudo-self interest of selfishness, and it appealed solely to the antisocial and brutal side of human nature." Furthermore, liberty or individuality did not in fact exist for a majority of people in a competitive society. Though nominally free, the poor were driven by the whip of hunger into making choices that they did not want. Even the rich were not totally insulated, because the insecurity of their rank had a similar effect. Obviously something of individuality had to be given up if society was to function in a collectivist frame of mind. But the message of *Looking Backward* was that people would attain true liberty by being relieved of the fear of want.

Bellamy offered a softened form of socialism, one that would be palatable to many middle-class readers of his day. *Looking Backward* may have been similar to Marxian theory in that it was the first utopian fantasy to reach the millennium along the new highways of historical and evolutionary theory, but Bellamy differed from the Marxists in at least one major respect: his theory did not depend upon, nor did it encourage, class conflict.

The confrontational posture that sprang from the Marxist attachment to class conflict provided good fuel for the warnings of laissez-faire theorists. If they needed testimony to show that the danger of revolution was more than a hallucination, Marxists like

Daniel DeLeon could be counted upon to provide it. Born in the Caribbean Islands and educated in Europe, DeLeon was at one point a lecturer at Columbia University. He took over the leadership of the Socialist Labor party in 1881 and remained as its head and the editor of its English-language weekly, *People*, until 1914. Admirers proudly called DeLeon "the uncompromising." Critics described him as a dogmatic idealist, a zealot, a doctrinaire who would make no compromise with principles.

These traits were conspicuous in his explanation of the idea of class conflict. "The capitalist class and labor," he said, "are enemies born." To him the claim that capital was the source of wealth was a cruel myth. He told laborers that "when, on pay day, you reach out your horney, unwashed hand it is empty. When you take it back again your wages are in it. Hence the belief that the capitalist is your source of living." Calling this an optical illusion, he claimed that the opposite was true. It was not the capitalist who supported the worker, but the worker who supported the capitalist. Wages were that part of the product of labor that the capitalist paid back to the worker. Because the entire product was the result of the worker's effort in the first place, that which the capitalist kept amounted to theft. Between the working class and the capitalist class, DeLeon concluded, there was an irrepressible conflict, a class struggle for life. To him the socialist revolution demanded unconditional surrender of the capitalist class.

Of course DeLeon was not the only voice of Marxism in the United States. There were others, such as Morris Hillquit, a Russian-born attorney who opposed DeLeon's leadership and was instrumental in causing a split in the Socialist Labor party in 1898. Eventually Hillquit and most of the anti-DeLeon socialist-laborites joined forces with the Social Democratic party, which, due to the presidential campaigns of Eugene Debs, was probably the best known of the American socialist organizations of the time.

Hillquit's tone was less inflammatory than DeLeon's, but his message was the same. He explained that class conflict was the dominant factor in historical development because each class sought to fortify its economic position by the strong arm of the state. Thus the state became an instrument of repression. He observed that, although the theorists of laissez faire lauded inequality, they in fact organized society, especially law, on the basis of a fictitious assumption that all citizens had equal power. The effect was that the law merely allowed the strong to exploit the weak. The goal, and the result of socialism, was that the state, being a product of class struggle, would vanish. Hillquit and socialists like Debs, no less than DeLeon, offered revolution to solve the problems of capitalism.

The Marxist view of society had one thing in common with laissez-faire-social Darwinian tradition: it did not have a place for reform legislation. DeLeon viewed reforms as "palliatives" and "insidious sops." Socialists are not reformers, they are revolutionists, he said. They do not propose to change forms, but rather to change the inner mechanism of society. Furthermore, he held that revolution could come only from the working class, and he lumped middle-class reformers, "pure and simple" labor leaders, and conciliatory socialists such as Hillquit into a single disdainful category of enemies that he called fakers. Hillquit again took a milder stance. But although he did not disdain or reject all partial reforms, he did not expect substantial relief from measures such as tenement-house reforms, factory laws, and child labor laws.

Laissez-faire theorists painted themselves as the mainstays of American heritage. They did not hesitate to warn of the threat to individualism and liberty—the specter of socialism—lurking in every attempt at legislative reform. Genuine though their concern might have been, when carried to the extreme this single-mindedness tended to confuse the issue. Political, economic, and social life in late nineteenth-century America was not that clear cut.

Laissez faire may have been the philosophy that transformed the United States into a modern industrial society, but as the century progressed many respected leaders and thinkers began to believe that its adherence to the negative state had outlived its validity. These people thought that changes in society had produced problems that could be solved only by people acting in concert through the organ of government. They realized that the result—legislation—was not necessarily the same thing as collectivism. Those who describe it as such, said one, "have never grasped the fundamental idea of modern democracy, which is that government is not something apart from us and outside of us, but we ourselves."

To some extent the failure to "grasp this fundamental idea," and much of the disagreement and confusion about the role of government, could be attributed to the fact that individualism holds a revered place in American heritage and American myth. An attachment to individualism is evident in the fundamental design of our Constitution, which set up a government of limited powers that derives its authority from the people. Individualism continued to be a major element in popular political philosophy throughout our early history. Prior to the Civil War, for example, it was reflected in the teachings of Jacksonian Democracy and the ideals of free-labor theory. There is no reason to think the attraction to individualism would have been abandoned as the nineteenth century drew to a close.

Even socialists would be compelled to recognize that it was an important factor behind the failure of their philosophy to become a major force in the American scene. Nineteenth-century workers by and large regarded themselves as free and equal individuals, each with a chance to improve his or her lot and attain the American dream. They were relatively willing to fight for higher wages, shorter hours, and other immediate goals, but were less inclined to embrace crusades based upon class struggle and collectivism.

This tradition of individualism may well have allowed Americans to feel comfortable with the language of laissez faire. However, it does not necessarily follow that the laissez-faire brand of individualism is the exact counterpart of that tradition or that people thought it best for each of them to be isolated in a struggle for pecuniary advantage. American comfort with the language of laissez faire may even have been enhanced by the fact that laissez-faire theorists possessed a common ancestry with our constitutional tradition, both having roots in classical liberalism. But, like most siblings, the two developed along somewhat different paths.

Historian Robert McCloskey offered one explanation of the difference. The central concern of democracy, he observed, is the morally free individual. Within its concept of liberty there are a number of subvalues, economic freedom being only one. William Graham Sumner's definition of liberty was, by contrast, materialistic and utilitarian. It guaranteed to all people the right to use their own power and product for their own welfare and was equated with competition, contract, and private property. Sumner and his followers had elevated the subsidiary value of economic freedom to the level of an end in itself—in fact, to the level of the primary end. In the process the moral and humane aspects of liberty were cast aside.

McCloskey suggested that nineteenth-century conservatives were able to remold the democratic faith and infuse its catchwords with entrepreneurial meanings. The latter part of this claim may well be true. For most Americans the word "liberty," for example, unquestionably includes the idea of controlling one's own property. But turn-of-the-century reformers, people such as those who were active in passing the Bakeshop Act, had not lost sight of the human aspects of liberty. They realized that economic liberty could not be absolute, and they believed that unfettered individualism could itself be the cause of lost freedom. The prevalence of economic regulation in the nineteenth century demonstrates that as a practical matter, the democratic faith had not been remolded to fit the laissez-faire ideal of the negative state. As a matter of fact, the theoretical view of political economics was not molded in that manner either. The influence of laissez faire–social Darwinism, both as a socioeconomic theory and as a political doctrine, had peaked by the 1870s and 1880s. Toward the end of the century, unwavering attachment to the negative state was being questioned even from within the laissez-faire camp.

Francis Amasa Walker, the son of laissez-faire economist Amasa Walker, was one economist who parted from some of the standard beliefs of his colleagues. Walker criticized their blind acceptance of a preconceived set of natural laws and their unrealistic model "economic man," who was driven by nothing other than the pursuit of wealth. He also recognized that perfect competition did not exist in reality, especially in the relationship between employer and employee. Realism led Walker to accept a limited role for the state. Perfect competition remained the ideal. Where it did not exist, however, legislation that would reduce the impact of inequality by providing a crutch for those who were less able to compete was acceptable.

The year 1885 saw the New York Court of Appeals deciding *In re Jacobs*, the cigar makers' case mentioned earlier in this chapter. That case is thought to be one of the first to use laissez-faire theory to interpret the law and is considered a major stepping-stone toward a more general use of the theory by the courts. Ironically that same year also saw the formation of an organization that signified that economic theory was already moving onto new ground. The organization was the American Economic Association, a brainchild of Richard T. Ely, Henry Carter Adams, Edmund J. James, and a group known as "the new school" of political economics.

Rejecting both the unrestrained competition of laissez faire and the collectivism of socialism, the new-school economists expressly favored state intervention in the economy. Like Francis Walker they observed that perfect competition did not exist in many spheres of the economy and that self-interest alone did not explain all economic acts. But in advancing the idea of the positive state, they took the next step of rejecting the idea that economics was a morally neutral science. The role of economics is not limited to "what is," they said, it also concerns itself with moral values. Its purpose, observed Ely, is to seek the welfare of society and to promote the welfare of the great mass of individuals. It followed that it was the duty of the state to take positive action in behalf of society's general well-being.

New-school economists were not the only theoreticians who favored the positive state. Other famous thinkers, such as Washington Gladden in theology, Frank Lester Ward in sociology, and William James in philosophy, also rejected the teachings of laissez-faire economists as well as those of Herbert Spencer and William Graham Sumner. In challenging the ideal of unrestrained competition and individualism, these people did not believe that they were threatening liberty. On the contrary, they believed that liberty had positive as well as negative aspects and that it could be restrained by the conditions of society as well as by an act of government. To them the question involved in this debate was not one of "liberty or no liberty," as Sumner had said. Rather it was one of how to define liberty and whose liberty was to receive precedence over another's when they came into conflict.

These people were simply talking about fairness. They believed that government existed not only to preserve liberty but also to promote justice. Furthermore, many were convinced that by ignoring fairness, the tenets of laissez faire–social Darwinism had as much to do with endangering liberty as did socialism. The extremes, they observed, fed off of each other. The desire for revolutionary change offered by socialism was the outcome of policies based upon doctrinaire individualism. "The existing tendencies toward Socialism," explained Washington Gladden, "are the natural fruit of Unsocialism."

Theorists and academics were not the only ones who were concerned about the possibility that policies based upon the doctrine of the negative state might provide an incubator for revolution. The National Civic Federation (NCF) was formed in 1900 for the express purpose of improving relations between labor and capital and avoiding conflict or radical change. Led by leaders of American business and labor as well as politicians and reformers, the NCF during the first quarter of the twentieth century was influential in promoting a program of moderate reform. It was a program that opposed what the organization considered to be twin threats to the American political and social system: socialism among the workers and the anarchy of laissez faire among other elements of the business community.

The laissez-faire–social Darwinian tradition was obviously an important part of nineteenth-century American thinking, and it continues to have an impact in the twentieth century. As the nation neared the turn of the century, however, it was just as obvious that a strong current of American intellectual thinking was moving in another direction. As early as 1884 Richard T. Ely was referring to laissez faire as "the past of political economy." Washington Gladden expressed the belief that laissez faire was out of date in another way, observing that, although "individualism had been a good club wherewith to fight feudalism, it is a bad corner-stone whereon to rear society." Political, economic, sociological, and philosophical thought in nineteenth-century America was not static. It was not dominated by laissez faire and social Darwinism. It was vibrant, varying, and changing.

Theoretical arguments about the role of the state undoubtedly found their way into legislative proceedings. It is important to realize, however, that legislatures are not guided by theoretical considerations alone. Their usual role requires finding practical solutions to specific problems, and the art of persuasion in that forum involves power or clout at least as much as it involves logic. The lack of available records makes it difficult to determine the extent to which theory came directly into play in the New York legislature's consideration of the Bakeshop Act in 1895. What is known is that the bakeshop law did not immediately attract wide attention. The issues that brought it to center stage revolved around the proper role of government. It was a direct confrontation between the idea of the negative state and an attempt at legislative reform. But the bakeshop law remained relatively obscure until it entered the judicial arena. Although this may have been simply a matter of circumstances, it is more likely that something about the judicial process itself and the impact of the Supreme Court's decisions drew attention to the case.

In the courtroom the issue of shorter-hours legislation was ostensibly removed from the context of practical politics. Theoretically the issue would be decided solely on legal principles, but it is possible that the legal atmosphere served mostly to make the issue conspicuous as a conflict between contrasting views of the state's role. In any event, with the shift to this new forum, the debate would be intensified by the addition of another issue. New York's Bakeshop Act was to become the center not only of a disagreement about the state's function but also of the judiciary's authority to determine that role. The way in which these two issues became intertwined is best explained through the progress of the case that tested the validity of the law—*Lochner v. New York.*

CHAPTER 7

Nothing to Do with Due Process

Joseph Lochner was an obscure owner of a small bakeshop in Utica, New York. A photograph of Lochner's bakery taken in 1908, a few years after his case in the U. S. Supreme Court, shows a relatively airy and mechanized aboveground shop quite unlike the typical urban bakeries described in Edward Marshall's exposés. It is possible that this photograph is misleading. Because changes in the bread-baking industry were occurring very rapidly during this time, Lochner's shop in 1908 may have been very different from his shop in 1902, when he was charged with violating the bakeshop law. It is also possible that Lochner's business was not typical of the time. Whatever the case, Mr. Lochner probably liked to think of himself as a respectable citizen and businessman. He therefore must have been somewhat perturbed when he saw his name emblazoned in the daily newspaper alongside those of a killer, a rapist, a thug, and assorted thieves whose criminal trials would be heard during the February 1902 term of the county court.

Lochner's legal problems arose because the state of New York had declared some of his business practices to be unlawful. Because he had either coerced or allowed one of his employees, a baker named Aman Schmitter, to work more than sixty hours in one week, he had broken the New York bakeshop law, which declared that no employee "shall be required, permitted or suffered" to work more than sixty hours in one week or more than ten hours in one day. If convicted, Lochner would be subject to a fine or imprisonment. This was not his first violation of that law, nor would it be his last. If nothing else, his continued disregard for the legal ceiling on working hours suggested that Joseph Lochner was a hardheaded man who had determined that no one else was going to tell him how to run his business—not the state of New York and especially not his workers or their union.

A long-standing feud between Lochner and the Utica branch of the journeyman bakers' union creates the suspicion that the union may have been behind his indictment; and that the state factory inspector, rather than Lochner's overworked employee Aman Schmitter, initiated the complaint serves to reinforce that suspicion. Soon after the bakeshop law was passed, the factory inspector joined forces with the union in an effort to assure compliance. Chief Factory Inspector James Connolly authorized union leader Henry Weismann to take affidavits from workers who complained of violations of the shorter-hours regulations. The union undoubtedly tried to use this authority to send a message to leaders of the Retail Bakers' Association, such as its president, Conrad Moll, or to recalcitrant shop owners, such as Lochner.

In the beginning, the union could brag about its success. Violations were found in one hundred five of the one hundred fifty bakeries inspected in New York in the three months after the law took effect. Four employers were arrested in Brooklyn. Within a few years, however, enthusiasm began to wane. Complaints about the difficulty of enforcing the law surfaced, just as they had in the wake of prior shorter-hours laws.

Some master bakers were outraged about the new law. In the first case to be reported, bakeshop owner Newton Burns was so abusive of the factory inspector that the trial judge had to warn him to treat the public official with more civility. Master bakers complained about the law and attempted to get amendments passed that would render it ineffective. They most assuredly hoped that the courts would overrule it. Given their opposition to the statute, the Retail Bakers' Association might have tried to find, or even create, a set of circumstances that would make a good court case against it. But there is nothing about Joseph Lochner's case to suggest that he was placed in jeopardy as part of a deliberate plan to nullify the Bakeshop Act. Unlike the famous cigar makers' case, which had overturned a significant reform law some twenty years earlier, Lochner's trial did not have the earmarks of a concocted test case.

The crime that Lochner had allegedly committed took place during the second week of April 1901; he was arrested and charged shortly thereafter. This was a misdemeanor, not a serious crime; but the procedure that New York used in handling such cases was the same. The first step was to send it to the grand jury. The duty of this body was to review the criminal cases presented to it by the district attorney in order to determine whether the evidence that a crime had been committed was sufficient to warrant making a formal charge. If it was, the grand jury had to state the specific charges in a document called an indictment, and the case went to court.

On October 22, about six months after his arrest, the grand jury of Oneida County indicted Joseph Lochner for violation of the Bakeshop Act, and a trial was scheduled for that term of the county court. Lochner's main defense, however, was actually offered before the trial ever started. In a pretrial hearing in November 1901 Lochner's attorney, William S. Mackie, asked for a dismissal on the grounds that the grand jury had not properly stated the charges against his client. It was a technical objection that if found to be valid would annul the indictment. Mackie also made another objection, one that probably struck the district attorney and judge as being somewhat vague but that came closer to his client's perception of the issues involved in his case. The facts stated in the indictment, Mackie argued, did not constitute a crime.

Trial judge W. T. Dunmore was not convinced. He denied the pretrial motions, and on February 12, 1902, the case went to trial. At the opening of the trial, when the judge asked him whether he wanted to plead guilty or innocent, Lochner refused to do either. He offered absolutely no defense to the charges made against him, giving Judge Dunmore no other choice but to find him guilty and sentence him to pay fifty dollars or spend fifty days in jail.

Lochner and his attorney had chosen simply to skip a level in the judicial process. They did not even attempt to win his case at trial and apparently had planned all along to appeal. This did not necessarily mean, however, that it was their intention to make this a test case by challenging the constitutional validity of the Bakeshop Act in the appeals courts. In fact, although Mackie's tactics assured that there would be an appeal, they were not a particularly adroit way to test the statute. By attacking the form of the indictment, Mackie left open a possibility for the appeals court to decide his client's fate on a technicality. It could absolve Lochner without even considering the claim that the statute was invalid. If the court did choose to look into that issue, Lochner's refusal to defend himself at the trial would also have been a mistake—that is, unless there were absolutely no circumstances in his favor.

Appeals courts do not hear evidence. Their function is to decide questions of law. The facts surrounding a case are theoretically determined at the trial. Yet even at the appellate level, facts are useful in placing questions of law within a worldly context and giving substance to abstract legal issues. When Joseph Lochner refused to plead, he also chose not to create a factual record for his side of the case.

If Joseph Lochner had been intent upon overruling the Bakeshop Act, his attorney could have used testimony at the trial to paint the statute in the most unfavorable light. Just as William M. Evarts had done in the cigar makers' case, he could have introduced evidence that would direct the appellate judges' attention to what he saw as the inequity, injustice, or inexpediency of the law. Instead he chose to rely on the dispassionate statement in the grand jury indictment charging that he had "permitted and required one Aman Schmitter, an employee in his employ, to work more than sixty hours in one week."

On the same day that his client was convicted, Mackie filed an appeal to the Appellate Division of the Supreme Court of New York. This court, comprising several regional departments, was the first level of appeal in New York State. Lochner's appeal was heard by five judges who sat on the bench of the Fourth Department, which was located in Rochester. The Appellate Division did not let Lochner off on a technicality. In fact, his attorney's argument that the indictment was defective was dismissed almost without comment. Mackie's vague claim at the pretrial hearing that the facts stated in the indictment did not constitute a crime had, however, left a crack through which he would now try to attack the validity of the statute.

As Mackie expanded upon this claim, it became evident that his theory was similar to that which had been successful in the cigar makers' case. Quoting from that case, he argued that "laws which impair or trammel the right of one to use his faculties in lawful ways, to earn his livelihood in any lawful calling, to pursue any lawful trade or avocation, are infringements upon his fundamental rights of liberty which are under constitutional protection." That might be so, agreed Judge John M. Davy in his majority opinion, but the bakeshop law was not a prohibition. It was merely a regulation, and as such it was a valid exercise of the state's power. Joseph Lochner's conviction was upheld by a vote of 3 to 2.

Following this defeat Lochner and Mackie decided to continue the process of appeal. They had found two sympathetic judges at the Appellate Division, and there were more waiting at the next court and highest level of appeal in the state, the New York Court of Appeals. One was Judge Dennis O'Brien, who, since his election to New York's highest court in 1889, had voted consistently against statutory reform. Judge O'Brien was in favor of overturning Lochner's conviction; in a written opinion, he took up where Mackie's argument had left off. Calling the Bakeshop Act "one of those paternal laws which must inevitably put enmity and strife between master and servant," he concluded that it was an unconstitutional infringement on the liberty of the parties. The act made it a crime for the employer to allow employees to work over the statutory time, he observed, regardless of the wants and necessities of the business or the desires of the workers. Unfortunately for Lochner, Judge O'Brien was not writing the opinion of the court. His comments were written in dissent from a 4 to 3 ruling that once again upheld Lochner's conviction.

One of the majority, Judge John Clark Gray, shared O'Brien's concern that there was a tendency toward excessive paternalism in government. Even though he thought that the statute was unwise, Gray voted with the majority because he believed that it was the legislature's duty to make that determination. The power resided in the legislature, he said, "and courts must presume that the legislative body was animated by a reasonable intention to promote the public welfare."

The opinion of the court was written by Chief Judge Alton Parker, who within a few months would be running against Theodore Roosevelt in a campaign for the presidency of the United States. Parker, a Democrat, was a favorite of New York boss David Hill. Much of his popularity among fellow party members came as a result of his first campaign for the chief judgeship in 1897. In a year when Democrats suffered defeat throughout the state, Parker won his contest by a large margin.

The 1904 presidential campaign showed that Parker was a better judge than presidential candidate. During the course of his career on the bench, he had developed a reputation as a competent and conservative jurist. Yet he also showed some sympathy for reform.

More than once he was pitted against Judge O'Brien in cases that concerned reform legislation. These tendencies toward both conservatism and reform continued when his judicial career was over. After being defeated overwhelmingly by Roosevelt, Parker went into private law practice. He represented the American Federation of Labor before a congressional subcommittee; on another occasion he defended Samuel Gompers, who had been charged with contempt of court for participation in a union boycott. Eventually Parker became president of the American Bar Association and then president of the National Civic Federation.

Parker agreed with Judge Gray that the bakeshop law was a legitimate exercise of the state's power. He went a step further, however, directly addressing the concern that Gray and O'Brien shared over the growing tendency toward paternalism in government. In our country's early history, he said, there was no need for special protection of particular classes of people. The need for this type of legislation had accompanied modernization. Regulations such as the Bakeshop Act did not amount to paternalism. On the contrary, they represented legitimate experiments by the state to deal with modern problems. The chief judge did not question the importance of individual liberty emphasized by Judge O'Brien. He merely maintained that this liberty was not absolute, that it must sometimes yield to the general welfare. "The individual," he said, "must sacrifice his particular interest or desires if the sacrifice is a necessary one in order that organized society as a whole be benefited."

The dispute that underlay this case before the New York Court of Appeals was a familiar one. Judge O'Brien, joined by two others, had attached himself to the concept of the negative state. Liberty, as he chose to define it, closely followed Herbert Spencer's law of equal freedom. And because the Bakeshop Act infringed upon that liberty, it was therefore invalid as a violation of the fundamental rights that the laws of nature granted to every individual. Chief Judge Parker, taking the position of mainstream reformers, disagreed that laissez-faire individualism ruled out the possibility of the state becoming involved in social and economic reform. The majority of the judges rejected at the very least the idea that the court had authority to do anything about the legislature's violation of laissez-faire precepts.

This time, however, the debate over the role of the state was not taking place in academic journals, the popular press, a political rally, or even in a state legislature. It was in a court of law. Theoretical and economic arguments, convincing though they might be, would not provide sufficient material for building a case. Those arguments had to be given legal substance and tied to legal concepts. Although each judge's philosophical points and predilections undoubtedly had some impact upon his opinion, the literal legal complaint made by Joseph Lochner was that the Bakeshop Act was an invalid deprivation of rights that were guaranteed to him by the Constitution of the United States.

Americans tend to be quick to demand their rights. The protest "That is unconstitutional!" is often used in everyday circumstances when no real reference to the Constitution is intended. When it is used in this manner the phrase represents nothing more than an expression of dissatisfaction and frustration. It means simply "I want to" or "That is unfair." Joseph Lochner complained that it was unconstitutional for the state to prohibit him from working his employees for as many hours as he, or they, wanted. Had he done so prior to 1868 his protest would have been little more than a meaningless tirade. It would have had absolutely no basis in the law. But by 1904, changes in constitutional law had given some legal substance to his contention.

The significance of 1868 was that the Fourteenth Amendment to the Constitution was ratified that year. This amendment, specifically its due process clause, furnished a wedge that was eventually used to expand the power of courts to invalidate state laws. It was manipulated so effectively by some members of the judiciary and legal profession that by the turn of the century, critics were complaining that it had created a virtual "judicial veto" over the acts of state legislatures.

The power of federal courts to declare state laws unconstitutional was not a new creation. It is implicit in the document itself, as a logical application of its declaration in Article 6 that the Constitution and laws of the United States shall be "the supreme law of the land." It was also expressly recognized when the first Congress of the United States passed the Judiciary Act of 1789. Defining the appellate jurisdiction of the Supreme Court, this act gave it the authority to review cases involving the constitutionality of certain state statutes. But even though judicial review of state legislation surely existed before the Fourteenth Amendment was adopted, it was applicable to only a few types of laws.

State laws that interfered with interstate commerce composed one such category. Article 1, section 8, of the Constitution, which gives Congress the power to regulate interstate commerce, was designed to facilitate trade among the states. The goal of the commerce clause was the creation of a "common market" under the protection of the national government. The Supreme Court was keeping that purpose in mind when, in some of the most important early cases, it nullified state statutes that tended to inhibit the free flow of interstate trade. When New York gave inventor Robert Fulton exclusive rights to operate steamboats on the Hudson River, for example, the Court saw it as a trade barrier and ruled that the law was unconstitutional. Similarly, a license that the state of Maryland required for importing goods from other states was set aside as an unconstitutional tariff.

State statutes that interfered with other functions that the Constitution gave to the federal government also came under judicial scrutiny. This was the issue in the famous case of *McCulloch v. Maryland*, which ruled that a state tax on the Bank of the United States was unconstitutional. It also came into play when, following the War of 1812, a Virginia law that confiscated property owned by British subjects was overruled because it conflicted with the exclusive right of the federal government to make treaties with foreign nations.

The only other laws for which judicial review was available were those that violated specific limitations on the power of the states found in Article 1, section 10, of the Constitution. The most significant of these is that "no state shall pass any law impairing the obligation of contracts." The rationale behind the contract clause was illustrated by an 1819 case that overturned a state law that released debtors from their existing liabilities. The clause meant simply that a state could not annul existing private obligations by an act of legislation. Nor could it release itself from its own prior contractual obligations. This is what Georgia legislators tried to do in 1795, when they repealed their predecessors' agreement to sell a vast tract of public land. Even though the earlier sale had been influenced by bribery, the Supreme Court overruled the repeal.

Instances in which the U.S. Supreme Court overruled acts of state legislatures were not uncommon during the first seventy-five years of the history of the Constitution. However, the scope of the Court's authority to do so was very narrow. Although the national government was recognized as supreme within its sphere of activity, that sphere included only powers that were enumerated in or implied by the Constitution. All other functions of government were left to the states. Not even the federal Bill of Rights applied to their activities.

This vast field of authority left to the states became known as the "police power," a term that was picked up from several opinions written by Chief Justice John Marshall. Marshall used it to distinguish functions of state governments from functions of the federal government under the commerce clause. It was a term of convenience so broad as to be virtually undefinable. "The police powers," Chief Justice Roger Taney later admitted, "are nothing more or less than that power of government inherent in every sovereignty to the extent of its dominion, the power to govern men and things." Used in this way, the term did not envision limitations on the activities of the states within their sphere of authority.

Given this traditional understanding, one would not suspect that the way in which the Supreme Court chose to define the police power would eventually become the key to Joseph Lochner's hopes to have the New York bakeshop law invalidated and his conviction reversed. By the time his case came to the Court, however, reference to the police power of the states carried an implication that was quite different from that emanating from its original use. No longer was it simply a linguistic means of drawing the line between state and federal activities. From a shortcut description of the breadth of state power it had become an integral part of a theory of law that severely limited the power of states to govern even within their own domain.

The springboard for this somersault in constitutional theory was a clause in the Fourteenth Amendment that guarantees that "no state shall . . . deprive any person of life, liberty, or property without due process of law." Although its very first words, "no state shall," show that the clause was written as a limitation on state authority, legal history has made it just as clear that it was not intended to be a wholesale restriction on the police power. The guarantee of due process did not originate with the Fourteenth Amendment. At the time the amendment was passed, a due process clause already existed in the Fifth Amendment to the United States Constitution. Due process clauses could also be found in the constitutions of every state of the union, although they were sometimes stated in another way— for example, that the state would not deprive one of life, liberty, or property except by "the law of the land."

This guarantee first appeared in the Magna Carta in 1215. Intended as a safeguard against the arbitrary and despotic exercise of executive power, due process had usually been understood to mean that government could not punish people without first giving them a fair hearing and an opportunity to prove themselves innocent. As such it had nothing to do with the content of legislation. It promised only that life, liberty, and property could not be taken from any person except through ordinary, established legal procedures.

If this had remained its meaning, the due process clause would have been of little value to Lochner or to any others who hoped to find a prohibition on state economic and social regulations within the Constitution. In the same year that the Fourteenth Amendment was ratified, however, a foundation was laid for a new and expanded version of due process. It came in the form of a legal treatise that was written by University of Michigan law professor and Michigan supreme court justice Thomas McIntyre Cooley. The very title of Cooley's book, *A Treatise on the Constitutional Limitations Which Rest upon the Legislative Powers of the States of the American Union*, provides a reliable indication of both its emphasis and its length. In the preface of *Constitutional Limitations*, Cooley claimed that it was not his intention "to advance new doctrines, or do more than state clearly with reasonable conciseness the principles to be deduced from judicial decisions." Perhaps his disclaimer reflected nothing more sinister than modesty, but Cooley was undeniably guilty of a slight misrepresentation, because advance a new doctrine is exactly what he did.

His unconventional position could be found in chapter 2, "Of Protection of Property by the Law of the Land." Due process of law, Cooley said, was more than a guarantee of correct judicial procedure. It also meant that legislation itself could not interfere with vested rights beyond what was allowed by "settled maxims of law" and safeguards for the protection of individual rights. In other words, for Cooley due process represented a limit upon the state's authority to pass laws that interfered with private property. This was the seed for a theory that, because of its concentration on the substance of legislation rather than the procedure by which the law was enforced, was to become known as substantive due process.

Cooley assumed rather than proved the validity of this proposition. He had little choice. At the time there was little legal precedent to support it. The United States Supreme Court had spoken of due process in this manner only once—in one of the most disastrous decisions in constitutional history, the *Dred Scott* case. As a matter either of oversight or of tact, Cooley ignored the statement made by Chief Justice Taney in that case—that an act of Congress depriving slaveholders of their property merely because they brought slaves into a particular state or territory "can hardly be dignified with the name due process of law."

Instead Cooley chose to begin his discussion by quoting an argument made to the Supreme Court by Daniel Webster in the *Dartmouth College* case of 1819. The meaning of due process, Webster had argued, "is that every citizen shall hold his life, liberty, property, and immunities under the protection of general rules which govern society. Everything which may pass under the form of [a legislative] enactment is not the law of the land."

Webster may have had a sound point, but he was not talking about a limitation on the content of state laws in general. He was claiming that by passing a law that specifically nullified the charter of a private college and took the institution for state use, New Hampshire had passed sentence rather than legislation. It had performed a quasi-judicial function and, in the process, had denied Dartmouth College the procedural guarantees that were part of the due process clause of the Fifth Amendment.

This was a gray area, in which the extension of the meaning of due process was infinitely more narrow than what Cooley would have in mind. Having passed a law that applied retroactively to one particular person or group, New Hampshire's legislature had done something that resembled a punishment rather than a rule. The line between the procedural guarantee of due process and the substance of the law had been blurred. Furthermore, the legislature had stepped onto judicial turf, which gave the courts considerable motivation for finding within the due process clause the authority to review the content of legislation. They would be swayed by a jealous interest in insulating their own function from legislative encroachment.

It is true, as some modern scholars have claimed, that the idea of substantive due process existed in American law before the Civil War. But at the time that his treatise was first published, Cooley could point to only a few scattered state court opinions to support his extension of due process to the substance of legislation. By popularizing the theory and giving it added legitimacy, *Constitutional Limitations* became one of the most influential publications in American law, and Cooley in turn became the high priest of a theory that revolutionized thinking about the power of state legislatures and the role of the courts. As if in testimony to its own impact, the book itself grew as successive editions were published for sixty years. Cooley's explanation of substantive due process became more polished with the passing of several editions. In the 1903 edition, chapter 1 had almost doubled in length, most of the growth being footnotes to court cases that had applied his theory. By the time lawyers were preparing the *Lochner* case for appeal, even scholars who were inclined to disagree with Cooley's theory were forced to recognize that substantive due process had been accepted by virtually every court in the United States.

It is an understatement to say that this reinterpretation expanded the conventional meaning of the due process guarantee. In reality, it dropped entirely the qualifying phrase "due process of law." The clause in effect now read, "No state shall deprive any person of life, liberty, or property." Of course, most laws place some imposition on a person's liberty or some restriction on the use of private property. There had to be some qualification to this prohibition against legislative interference, but now it was undefined. It was left up to the subjective judgment of the courts to determine what was and what was not a legitimate exercise of the police power of the states.

How the idea had grown! In adopting substantive due process, the judicial branch was doing much more than protecting its own authority. It now assumed that it had the right to reign over the legislative domain of states. Another front had been opened—the courtroom joined the legislative chambers as a place to do battle over state regulation.

In this arena the concept of the police power carried its restyled significance. Courts would be determining whether statutes represented a legitimate exercise of the authority of states to interfere with the liberty of their citizens. The police power now became the concept that described the extent as well as the limitations of that authority. The validity of state laws was thus likely to depend upon how courts chose to define the boundaries of police power.

––––––

In the 1870s and 1880s, when the popularity of laissez faire and the belief in the negative state were at a peak, Cooley's emphasis on the limitations of state power filled a niche. It was quickly embraced by those in the legal profession who were opposed to the rising tide of legislative regulation of personal and, more particularly, property rights. At the same time, ratification of the Fourteenth Amendment provided a unique opportunity to put the theory into practice.

This amendment was one of three "reconstruction amendments" that were written to remedy specific problems that grew out of the aftermath of the Civil War. The first of these amendments, the Thirteenth, abolished slavery. Soon after it was ratified in 1865, however, it became apparent that this proclamation was not enough. Southern states responded with statutes, known as black codes, that used vagrancy and other misdemeanor laws, along with abbreviated judicial procedure, to return former slaves to what was virtually an indentured status. Section 1 of the Fourteenth Amendment, which includes the due process clause, was intended to eliminate such practices. (The last of these was the Fifteenth Amendment, which was ratified in 1870. It provided that the right to vote shall not be denied on account of race, color, or previous condition of servitude.)

The pertinent part of the Fourteenth Amendment reads:

No State shall make or enforce any law which shall abridge the privileges or immunities of citizens of the United States; nor shall any State deprive any person of life, liberty, or property, without due process of law; nor deny to any person within its jurisdiction the equal protection of the laws.

The framers of the amendment obviously chose broad language to accomplish their purpose. As a consequence, the meaning of the due process section has been the subject of debate for over one hundred years. One thing is certain, however: although the authors of the section wanted to limit the power of states, they were apparently not even thinking about the theory of the negative state or regulatory legislation in general. Their attention was focused on the problem at hand. It was not their collective intention to create a conduit for the transmission of laissez-faire theory into the Constitution.

One member of the committee that drafted the amendment may have been that farsighted, at least according to his own recollection. Seventeen years after it was ratified, acting as counsel for Southern Pacific Railroad, former senator Roscoe Conkling tried to convince the Supreme Court that this was indeed the secret intention of the committee all along. Subsequent research revealed that Senator Conkling's intimations were untrue and proved what common sense would have suggested: that it was unlikely that any legislative body would plan such a conspiracy and even more amazing to think that politicians had the discipline to keep the conspiracy a secret for almost twenty years. Nevertheless, the Fourteenth Amendment was a new law. What better place would there be for enterprising lawyers to sow original theories of the Constitution?

The argument made by one lawyer in the first Supreme Court case that dealt with the amendment is illustrative. The attorney was John A. Campbell, a former justice of the United States Supreme Court and one of the most respected lawyers of his time. The case, which became known as the *Slaughter-House Cases*, involved a Louisiana law that prohibited the operation of slaughterhouses in New Orleans except for one section on the edge of town set aside for that purpose. The legislature gave the Crescent City Live Stock Company the right to build and operate public slaughterhouse facilities on the site and also fixed the fees the company could charge butchers who used the facilities. A group of butchers who were dissatisfied with this arrangement filed a complaint in the state courts. They took it to the Supreme Court of Louisiana and lost. Now their last chance to obtain a reversal was to appeal to the Supreme Court of the United States.

Campbell knew that there was no precedent for the Supreme Court to interfere with this type of state legislation, but he was more imaginative than most lawyers. Although he did not seize upon the theory that would eventually become the basis for such interference, he did recognize that the butchers' only hope lay in the post–Civil War amendments. Thus he did what any groping lawyer might have done. Not knowing exactly what would work, he chose the scattergun tactic of making every argument that he could think of.

Campbell claimed that the statute violated the Thirteenth Amendment by reducing the butchers to a state of indentured servitude. The protections of the Fourteenth Amendment, he said, were not confined to former slaves. The amendment had completely altered the power of the states. Taken as a whole, it was designed to secure individual liberty, individual property, and individual security and honor from arbitrary, partial, proscriptive, and unjust legislation of state governments. Almost as an afterthought he claimed that his clients' property had been destroyed "not by due process of law, but by a grant of privilege to the favored [company]."

The majority of the Court disagreed. Campbell's interpretation of the Fourteenth Amendment was a great departure from the structure and spirit of our institutions, wrote Justice Samuel F. Miller. It would radically change the whole theory of state and federal relations and fetter state governments in the exercise of powers that have been universally conceded to them. The majority was convinced that no such results were intended by the Congress that proposed the amendment, nor by the legislatures of the states that ratified it. The pervading purpose of the amendment, Miller explained, "[was] the freedom of the slave race, the security and firm establishment of that freedom, and the protection of the newly-made freeman and citizen from the oppressions of those who had formerly exercised dominion over him." The disgruntled butchers probably found little comfort in the fact that their defeat had been by a 5 to 4 vote. The closeness of the decision, however, showed that Campbell had effectively initiated a movement for change. A dissenting opinion by Justice Stephen J. Field was of particular significance, especially as a preview of the role that he was destined to play.

Field was one of nine siblings in an extraordinary family. As children of a stern New England preacher, they started with little advantage in life except for their own intelligence, discipline, and perseverance. Yet four of them were to become powerful and famous figures. David Dudley Field was a successful lawyer and behind-the-scenes figure in New York and national politics. Cyrus was an entrepreneur who laid the first transatlantic cable. Matthew was a respected engineer and bridge builder. Stephen, who sat on the Supreme Court of the United States for thirty-four years, was certainly not the underachiever of the family.

His path to the Supreme Court led from his brother's New York law office, via the Isthmus of Panama, to the gold rush in California, where he began a tumultuous life, equal to any Hollywood version of the Old West. Almost penniless when he arrived in California, he quickly made a fortune by speculating in real estate. He ended up in a boomtown called Marysville, where after three days of residence he was elected alcalde, or justice of the peace, over an "old-timer" who had been there all of six days.

Having few other tools to work with, Field carried out his courtroom duties using his own version of frontier justice. Because there was no jail in Marysville and lynching had been the common penalty for robbery, he considered it lenient to have thieves whipped and banished from the community. Innovation was also his style in civil matters as he reconciled squabbling marriage partners and arbitrated property disputes. From the judicial office of alcalde, Stephen Field provided most of what little government the town had in its early days. It was the beginning of a political career that took him to the state legislature and then to the California Supreme Court, a career that connected him with some of the most powerful entrepreneurs of the West Coast, most notably railroad baron Leland Stanford.

Stanford unquestionably had a hand in convincing President Lincoln to appoint Field to the United States Supreme Court, and his efforts were rewarded as, time and time again, Justice Field voted to limit the power of states to regulate business. Nothing insidious need be made of the connection, however. These men shared the same background. Their success in the anarchy that was early California required strength, adaptability, and courage, doused with an ample amount of luck. Surely in their own minds, this was survival of the fittest. They were naturals to be attracted to the philosophy of Spencer and Sumner.

Field wasted no time in finding that philosophy in the new amendments to the Constitution. His dissent in the *Slaughter-House Cases* closely followed the argument made by Campbell. Relying on vague principles of "abstract justice" and "the liberty of citizens to acquire property and pursue happiness," he made the general claim that the amendments protected citizens of the United States against deprivation of their common rights by state legislation. However, it did not take long for him to see the power of Thomas M. Cooley's line of thinking and to settle on the due process clause as the method for attaching the theory of the negative state to the Constitution. In a concurring opinion less than one year later, Field asserted that a state prohibition on the sale of liquor had the effect of confiscating the property of a brewer and therefore deprived him of that property without due process of law.

What is more striking is how quickly Field's opponents on the Court acquiesced, at least in principle, to the idea that the due process clause gave them the right to review the substance of state legislation. For all practical purposes, it happened in the next major case in which the issue came up—an 1877 controversy that tested the constitutionality of state regulation of the rates charged by Chicago grain elevators. The majority opinion in that case made it plain that the pertinent question would not be whether the due process clause gave the Court that right, but rather under what circumstances it would be exercised.

The case, *Munn v. Illinois,* was an extension of a struggle between farmers and railroads. By the 1870s railroads had become the United States' primary commercial link. Because they provided the route to markets, corporate decisions about where to provide service and what to charge had a tremendous impact on the prosperity of rural localities. Railroads usually took full advantage of this power. Frustrated by high fares and discriminatory rates, farmers in the western states organized into societies known as the Granger movement. The Grangers were successful in pressuring legislatures to pass regulatory statutes in several midwestern states, including Illinois.

In the nineteenth-century American heartland, all roads led to Chicago. Much of the grain produced in the West and Midwest made its way to that city's waterfront. From there it was shipped through the Great Lakes and St. Lawrence River to the East Coast or directly to Europe. Chicago had become the greatest grain market in the world. All of the grain that arrived there was stored in fourteen immense elevators owned by nine business firms; cooperation among the firms allowed them to fix the price that they charged for storage. In 1871 the state of Illinois stepped in. As part of the Granger laws, it imposed a maximum charge for storage and handling of grain in Chicago.

The firm of Munn and Scott, which had been convicted of charging illegally high rates, was represented in its appeal by William C. Goudy and John N. Jewett. Both were skilled and prominent lawyers, and each had served as president of the Chicago Bar Association. The heart of their argument was that Illinois rate regulation was a bold attempt by the state to control the capital, property, and labor of a private individual. It amounted to nothing less than a confiscation of the elevator owner's property, they argued, and certainly was the type of action envisioned by the Fourteenth Amendment prohibition against taking of property without due process of law. Justice Field agreed. Once again he would be writing a dissent, but in this case he gained a significant concession.

Chief Justice Morrison Waite, who wrote the majority opinion, did not disagree with the proposition that the due process clause could protect private property from state regulation. Instead he adroitly negated its impact. Referring back to English common law, he pointed out that traditionally when private property is "affected with a public interest" it ceases to be purely private and becomes subject to regulation. The transformation occurred, he said, "when the property is used in a manner to make it of public consequence and affects the community at large." Given such a broad definition of public purpose, it is hard to imagine any circumstance in which regulation of economic matters would be prohibited. Certainly the regulation of railroads and grain elevators was not one.

Capable though Waite may have been as a chief justice, he was not known as a writer of lucid opinions. He once admitted as much in a letter to Justice Field, saying, "The difficulty with me is that I cannot give the reasons as I wish I could." So it was with his opinion in *Munn v. Illinois*. Although the public-purpose doctrine served him well for the moment, it carried the air of being an exception to the general rule. In this way it obscured a deeper difference between his opinion and Field's. Their disagreement was not merely over how deeply a business must step into the public realm in order to become subject to regulation. It was a matter of the fundamental nature of the powers given to the states. The difference of opinion about what those powers were lay at the heart of every due process case that was to come, and it generated the storm that eventually swirled around *Lochner v. New York*.

"When a person becomes a member of society," wrote Waite, "he necessarily parts with some rights or privileges which, as an individual not affected by his relations to others, he might retain." This circumstance was the source of the police powers of states, he continued, and under that power "the government regulates the conduct of its citizens . . . and the manner in which each shall use his own property, when such regulation becomes necessary for the public good."

In the eyes of Chief Justice Waite, Justice Miller, and others, promotion of the "public good" or "general welfare" represented the traditional and proper application of the police power. It was an expansive view of state authority, one that could probably encompass almost anything that a legislature might want to regulate. The lack of a more precise definition eventually became troublesome to Waite and Miller. Instead of holding to the original use of the phrase as a demarcation of federal authority, they had compromised with Field, making the police power a way of describing limitations on a state's control of its internal affairs. In this manner the expansive definition became inadequate. Now, in the absence of any general test, they were left with applying the limitations on a case-by-case basis.

It was obvious that Field would find Waite's capacious definition of the police power to be objectionable. His dissent in *Munn* revealed an unabashed distrust of democracy and the legislative process. "If this be sound law," he objected, "if there be no protection, either in the principles upon which our republican government is founded, or in the prohibitions of the Constitution against such invasion of private property, all property and all business in the state are held at the mercy of a majority of its legislature."

Justice Field did not suggest that the due process clause interfered with a state's right to exercise the police power. Rather, he proposed a very narrow definition of what that power encompassed. The language often used to describe the police power presented it as an undefined and irresponsible element of government, Field complained. He agreed that the police power could embrace an almost infinite variety of laws, but explained that it existed only to secure certain limited objects. "Whatever affects the peace, good order, morals, and health of the community," he said, "comes within its scope."

Standing alone, the words "peace" and "good order" do not seem to signal a narrow view of state power, but Field had something very restrictive in mind when he used them. The state may control the use and possession of a person's property, he declared, "only so far as may be necessary for the protection of the rights of others, and to secure to them the equal use and enjoyment of their property." Once again the influence of laissez faire–social Darwinism was readily apparent. Peace and good order simply signified the law's role of protecting property and providing rules for the settlement of disputes between owners of property. A state law requiring railroads to maintain fences along their lines or be liable for double damages to farmers whose stock wandered onto the tracks, for example, could thus represent a proper exercise of the police power. On the other hand, laws that placed a ceiling on prices charged by railroads and grain elevators, laws that sought to regulate giant businesses, assure fairness in labor relations, or alleviate hardships of poverty, or any attempt by government to alter the social or economic order, would not. With a few minor lapses, Field stuck with this definition for the remainder of his career. The only exceptions to his commitment to governmental non-interference lay in his willingness to accept state involvement in matters of public health and morals.

In an era marked by the discovery of bacteria and an ever-increasing awareness of infectious diseases, it is understandable that health regulations providing for quarantine and compulsory vaccination regulations could be viewed, even by proponents of laissez faire, as acceptable intrusions on individual liberty. Although it was a limited concession, this concern for public health and safety grew into a pronounced appendage to the laissez-faire definition of the police power. If the public was endangered by the possibility of fire, for example, a city ordinance that forbade the night operation of laundries, most of which were located in neighborhoods dominated by wooden buildings, was a valid exercise of the police power. This interpretation opened the door for a limited degree of regulation of employer-employee relations in dangerous occupations, and in early dangerous-trade cases, Field flashed a sign of concern for the welfare of employees themselves. State intervention was most clearly acceptable, however, when jobs, such as those of railroad conductors and engineers, involved the safety of the public.

Field's idea of the laws that a state could enact to guard the morals of the community was nothing more than an expression of puritan morality. He accepted prohibition and regulation of alcoholic beverages, lotteries, gambling, and prostitution, and he allowed Sunday closing laws. Field did not mean, however, that the state could interfere with an individual's liberty or property through laws that were intended to enhance morality in any broader sense. The idea of passing laws designed to promote justice, duty, loyalty, or good citizenship, for example, was clearly not what Field had in mind.

It is unlikely that Francis Wayland, Arthur Latham Perry, Edward Atkinson, Herbert Spencer, or William Graham Sumner would have been totally satisfied with this description of state authority. Field was willing to give a certain amount of policy discretion to state legislatures, but his definition of the police power came as close to a constitutional expression of laissez faire–social Darwinism or the negative state as these men could have hoped for. There is little doubt that this was his intention and that he viewed the Court as the guardian of their brand of individualism. Other members of the legal profession may have pressed for the Fourteenth Amendment's absorption of laissez faire–social Darwinism with more vigor or directness, but Field's position on the high court for a record thirty-four years placed him at the center of the effort.

When Stephen J. Field resigned from the bench in 1897, the popularity of laissez faire was ebbing. An element of the legal community had joined economists Richard T. Ely and Henry Carter Adams and other philosophers, sociologists, and professionals in expressing concern over both its harshness and its implications. Those who opposed the absorption of laissez faire into the Constitution would be faced with the incomplete legacy Field had left behind. He had been successful in convincing the Court to accept the idea of substantive due process, but the full implications of his limited definition of the police power had not yet been realized.

The opportunity would arise eight years later, when Joseph Lochner brought his case to the Supreme Court. This time, however, it would not be one of the great corporate lawyers of the era nor a leader of the American bar who made the laissez-faire argument. Lochner's counsel was not a William M. Evarts, a John A. Campbell, a William D. Guthrie, or a John N. Jewett. He was Henry Weismann: the same Henry Weismann who ten years earlier, as leader of the New York bakers' union, had urged his comrades to agitate for the eight-hour law.

CHAPTER 8

Freedom to Agree to Anything

Henry Weismann was jubilant and proud when Governor Levi P. Morton signed the New York Bakeshop Act into law. "The second of May, 1895," he crowed, "will forever stand forth as one of the most memorable days in the history of the great struggle of American bakers for better and more humane conditions." Who would have guessed that he would eventually be on the opposite side, arguing before the Supreme Court that the law's ten-hour workday was unfair to employers? Weismann had undoubtedly gone through a thorough transformation. But by the time the case came to court, this was probably what those who had dealt with him had come to expect.

Although Weismann had been the lobbyist for the journeyman bakers' union when the law was passed, he was only the editor of the organization's newsletter, not its official leader. Riding his success in the legislative session, however, he quickly displaced George L. Horn as the union's highest officer, international secretary. In June 1895 Horn resigned. The executive committee then voted to "amalgamate" the offices of international secretary and editor of the *Bakers' Journal* into one new post, which Weismann graciously agreed to fill. He was thus handed control of the organization without having to deal with the messy technicality of a vote by the general membership.

Weismann held on to that control for only two years. In the autumn of 1897, complaining of steady and unbearable antagonism and secret vilifications, he resigned. Opponents, who had forced him out, charged that he had been caught with his hand in the till. Eight months later, they offered what they thought to be conclusive evidence of a scheme in which Weismann and several others received kickbacks from the company that printed the *Bakers' Journal* and skimmed off some of the money paid by advertisers. The belated release of this evidence is probably explained by the fact that

Weismann's resignation led to a struggle for control of the union and possibly a battle for its very existence. Weismann was ushered out of office in much the same way he had come in. With the backing of a majority of the eleven-member executive committee, Weismann's former assistant editor, John Schudel, summarily announced that he was taking charge of the union and the *Bakers' Journal.* Schudel, however, was not able to sever cleanly the former leader's connection with the union, which was to be a source of problems for the union in the future.

Either at the end of his time in office or shortly thereafter, Weismann opened a bakery of his own. Having become a boss baker, he soon joined forces with his old enemies in the Retail Bakers' Association in a plan to pass a law that would water down the Bakeshop Act. Relying on Weismann's stature as a former union leader, they also proposed the creation of an independent bakers' union to represent the interests of both owners and employees of small bakeshops.

Weismann was probably still identified as a labor leader by many union members and legislators. More important, he retained contacts with businesses that advertised in the *Bakers' Journal,* as well as support within the union's executive committee. His initial plan, according to opponents, was to swing a few more members of the executive committee to his side, take over the union, and transform it into the new joint organization. It was a crafty strategy. Even if it failed, the internal strife that it would create was likely to work to Weismann's benefit. The distracted union leaders would be less capable of opposing amendments to the Bakeshop Act and would be more vulnerable to competition from a rival organization. Nevertheless, Weismann's plan failed on all counts. The Bakeshop Act and the journeyman bakers' union both remained intact. When the incident was over, Weismann became editor of the official publication of the Retail Bakers' Association, the *Bakers' Review.*

Years later, at the conclusion of the *Lochner* case, Weismann attempted to justify his defection. "The truth of the matter," he told the *New York Times,* "is that I have never been in sympathy with the radicals in the labor movement." Taking another approach, he claimed that upon becoming a master baker he had undergone "an intellectual revolution." There is no question, however, that Weismann not only rejected radicals but also forsook his friends in the labor movement.

His subsequent activities give the impression that any transformation in Weismann's attitude toward the ten-hour workday was as likely to be attributable to a malleable social conscience as to a revelation.

Putting his labor activism behind him, Weismann turned his attention to New York Republican politics. He had no doubt made political connections during the drive to enact bakeshop reform; but his main ticket for entry into the world of politics, and the one constant thread in his career, was his bilingual skill and German heritage. In 1900 he was named chairman of the German-American McKinley-Roosevelt League. In the next year's mayoral election, he backed the fusion ticket and took the speaker's platform in support of Seth Low. Victory for the anti-Tammany forces that year led to his appointment as chief deputy to the clerk of Kings County, a post that he occupied until 1903.

Except for the attention that came his way as a result of the Supreme Court's decision in *Lochner*, Weismann dropped out of the public light after 1901. However, he remained active in various German-American organizations. Then, as the nation was considering entry into World War I, his name suddenly resurfaced. Acting as president of the United German Societies of Brooklyn, and later as a member of the Friends of Peace, Weismann became a vocal advocate of American neutrality in the war. When the Friends of Peace came together in a Chicago convention on Labor Day of 1915, Weismann was named chairman of the resolutions committee. From its very opening the convention was sidetracked by the problem of refuting charges that the group represented Germany's interest rather than the desire for peace. American Federation of Labor (AFL) president Samuel Gompers was one of the people making those charges. Gompers, who eventually threw his weight behind American participation in the war on the side of the Allies, had publicly stated that the efforts of the society were in the interest of one of the warring nations.

The only course left open to the pacifists was to attack. Calling Gompers "a foe of labor," they threatened to wrest control of the AFL from him. This attack once again pitted Weismann against a former labor ally. Early in his career he had stood by Gompers and "pure and simple unionism" when radicals challenged the AFL president's leadership. Weismann's participation in this attack on Gompers carries no strong implications about his loyalty. The prospects of entry into the war caused many former friends to choose opposite sides. But there is one incident from Weismann's earlier involvement in German-American organizations that speaks more clearly than any other of his propensity to argue from either side of the fence. In 1912 this man who had made his first small mark in history as an opponent of Chinese immigration complained to President Taft of a bill in Congress that was likely to limit the immigration of Germans. Representing himself as the chairman of the National German-American Alliance, Weismann said, "We feel that attempts for further restrictions of immigration violate the traditions as well as the principles upon which our free country has been reared, and both from the point of view of humanity as well as sound economic policy they should be discouraged."

Henry Weismann claimed that after his falling out with the bakers' union, he studied law on the side while operating two bakeries. At the turn of the century, people who wanted to become lawyers did not have to attend an accredited law school. The necessary education could be obtained by "reading" in the office of an established attorney. Prospective lawyers eventually had to pass some examination, which was typically administered by a judge. Those who were successful were then admitted to the bar.

This was the only path to the legal profession that would have been open to Weismann. It was not an unusual route. Some of the greatest attorneys of the era had taken it; but most "read the law" only after they had completed a college education, and they did so in the offices of a prominent law firm. Weismann was definitely not among the elite when it came to his training. He had no formal education, and there is no record of where he read the law.

In fact, Weismann may have taken the step into legal practice somewhat prematurely. In 1901 he was accused of unauthorized practice of law. When the accusation was made by the opposing lawyer in a minor case, Weismann admitted that he was not certified to practice law but denied that he was "sailing under false colors." His appearance at that trial and several others, he explained, was only as a representative for Carl Shurz, president of the Legal Aid Society. Nothing serious came of the charge; but no record exists that Weismann was at that time, or any time thereafter, admitted to the bar in New York State. It seems that when he argued Joseph Lochner's case in the nation's highest tribunal, Henry Weismann was not licensed to practice law. At the very least the 1901 incident provided an indication of his stature in the legal community. Only a short time before his appearance in the Supreme Court, he was a law clerk handling minor offenses in a Brooklyn police court.

There is no way to know for sure just how Weismann got involved in the *Lochner* case or who originated the idea of appealing the decision of the New York Court of Appeals. Weismann claimed that the Retail Bakers' Association wanted to challenge the law and came to him. It is just as likely, however, that he planted the idea. Weismann had influence among the master bakers and a grudge against the journeyman bakers' union. He certainly knew enough about the statute and the circumstances surrounding its enactment, and he may have thought that the presence of a former supporter of the law as counsel for the opposition might sway some of the justices. Win or lose, handling an appeal to the Supreme Court of the United States would do much to enhance his reputation. In any event there is little doubt that it was Weismann who started the appeal moving and that he was the force behind the case.

His inexperience was evident in the first stages of the appeal. Appeals in this type of case were started with a document called a writ of error. This was simply an order that granted the right to appeal and directed the clerk of the trial court to send the record of the case to the Supreme Court. As legal procedure goes, it was a very informal process. No special form or style of petition was essential, and time limits were generous; but there were a few basic requirements. The party making the request was required to include in the petition a list of reasons for the appeal, called an assignment of error; to post bond; and to give the opponents notice of the intent to appeal. Finally, it was essential that the writ of error actually be granted and issued.

When Weismann took over the case, he asked Lochner's former attorney, William S. Mackie, to file with the state court a document entitled "Undertaking on Appeal to the United States Supreme Court." There was nothing improper about starting the appeal in the state court. Supreme Court rules provided that the petition for writ could be filed in lower state or federal courts or in the Supreme Court. The unusual title of Weismann's document was not fatal to the appeal either.

The document itself would have been, however, if it had not been corrected. Initially it declared an intention to appeal and post a bond of one hundred dollars. However, it did not include an assignment of error; more amazingly, it did not even request that a writ of error be issued by the court. Without this, there would be no order directing the county clerk to send the records to the Supreme Court. The appeal simply would not be started. Weismann's poorly crafted document, and his client's one-hundred-dollar bond money, would have sat in a file at the office of the Oneida County clerk—forever.

Inexperience notwithstanding, Weismann faced one major obstacle to taking this case up on appeal. He was not a member of the bar of the United States Supreme Court. In order to be eligible he would have had to have been admitted to practice in his own state for at least three years, and as late as June 29, 1901, he had admitted that he was not an attorney in New York. Either for this reason or because he recognized his own limitations, Weismann secured the help of Brooklyn lawyer Frank Harvey Field.

Politics probably played a part in bringing Field and Weismann together, because both were active in the Brooklyn Republican party. Like Weismann, Field supported Seth Low in his 1897, 1901, and 1903 campaigns for mayor of New York. While Weismann was serving as deputy clerk of Kings County, Field was chairman of the Brooklyn Campaign Committee for the Citizens' Union. Educated at Columbia Law School and a member of the American Bar Association as well as the New York State, New York City, and Brooklyn Bar Associations, Field was undoubtedly a more established and respected attorney than was Weismann. He was not, however, one of the more colorful lawyers of the time. In fact, his practice attracted the attention of the press on only one occasion: later in his career, he and several other members of the board of deacons attempted to oust the pastor of Brooklyn's Washington Avenue Baptist Church. Nor did Field have a great deal of experience at the Supreme Court. His only prior case at that level came in 1902, when he was associated with former judge and legal writer Seymour D. Thompson in a losing effort to appeal the assessment of a state tax on a Brooklyn bank.

Although Weismann probably remained the driving force behind the *Lochner* case and was eventually granted special permission to appear before the Court, he officially assumed the supporting status "of counsel." With Field on board, the whole appeal procedure was started over. A proper petition and order for writ of error was filed in the Supreme Court and was granted by Justice Rufus W. Peckham. One minor logistical problem remained. Joseph Lochner still had one hundred dollars of bond money filed in the Oneida County clerk's office. Rather than forcing him to pay another bond, Justice Peckham informally solved that problem by giving Weismann and Field a few days to arrange to have the money transferred. With the procedural requirements thus satisfied, Joseph Lochner's appeal to the Supreme Court of the United States was under way.

It did not take a great deal of experience to determine that the odds in favor of the Supreme Court's overturning New York's ten-hour law were not very good. Lochner's attorneys may have found some encouragement in the fact that the Court was generally thought of as the bulwark of conservatism and the enemy of reform. In the previous decade, Supreme Court decisions had denied the federal government the power to levy an income tax, undermined the Sherman Antitrust Act, given its blessing to the antiunion device of the labor injunction, and watered down the Interstate Commerce Act. But if Weismann and Field did not know it when they began the case, they must have soon realized that the Court's reputation was not earned as a result of interpretation of the Fourteenth Amendment's due process clause. Admittedly the Court had adopted substantive due process as a general proposition. It had assumed the power to invalidate state economic regulation and reform legislation. Yet even though it had been asked to do this in hundreds of cases since the *Slaughter-House* decision, on only a few occasions had it ruled that such a state law was unconstitutional.

One area in which the laissez-faire interpretation of due process did have substantial impact was in state attempts to regulate the rates and services of railroads. In 1896 the Supreme Court invalidated a Nebraska statute that had given the state board of transportation the power to force the Missouri Pacific Railroad to allow a farmers' cooperative to build a grain elevator on its right of way. Two years later, the Court invalidated a Nebraska rate regulation. It negated the effect of *Munn v. Illinois* by ruling that rate ceilings that did not permit a "fair rate of return on invested property" violated the Fourteenth Amendment prohibition against taking property without due process of law.

These decisions stretched the concept of property to include not only tangible things but also the potential for profit. The impact that a state law limiting the length of a workday might have on profits was more remote, however, and to claim that it would also deprive people of their property was stretching the definition of that term almost to the breaking point. But there was a theory of law that Lochner's lawyers could base their case upon, a theory by which substantive due process could be applied to regulations of the relationship between employer and employee or almost any other social or economic legislation. It is called liberty of contract.

The name given to this theory could cause it to be confused with the contract clause, but they are distinctly different. The contract clause, which is one of the specific prohibitions on the power of the states found in Article 1, section 10, of the Constitution, prohibits states from passing laws "impairing the obligation of contracts." This guarantees the sanctity of a contract that has already been made. Liberty of contract, on the other hand, refers to the freedom of two or more people to make any agreement that they might desire. Like substantive due process, the liberty-of-contract theory is nowhere to be found in the Constitution or in its interpretation prior to the Civil War.

Also like substantive due process, the theory owed much of its credibility to the opinions of Justice Stephen J. Field. Beginning with his dissent in the *Slaughter-House Cases*, Field melded the concepts of liberty and property—both protected by the Fourteenth Amendment—to come up with "the right to pursue an ordinary trade or calling." This embryo of liberty of contract was not based upon the Constitution but rather upon natural rights—at least the version of natural rights expounded by laissez-faire economists. A footnote at the end of his opinion made it clear that the keystone of Field's theory was Adam Smith's proposition that labor is the original foundation of all property and that interference with the use of that labor was therefore "a manifest encroachment upon the just liberty both of the workman and those who might be disposed to employ him."

Field's argument had roots that were imbedded in American soil far deeper than laissez faire–social Darwinism. Modern historians have reminded us that this idea of liberty of contract is linked to a "free-labor ideology" that was the heart of the abolitionist movement. They have pointed out that opposition to "class legislation" and "special legislation" had been part of Anglo-American political philosophy since long before the Declaration of Independence. But it was a particular brand of free-labor ideology that Field was espousing. If his bond with laissez-faire–social Darwinian thought was not made evident enough by the *Slaughter-House Cases* footnote, it became more so a decade later in another case involving New Orleans butchers. Finding support for his idea in the Declaration of Independence, Field observed that the right to pursue happiness means "the right to pursue any lawful business or vocation in any manner not inconsistent with the equal rights of others which may increase their prosperity and develop their faculties." It was as if he had laid a page of the *United States Supreme Court Reports* over *Social Statics* and traced Herbert Spencer's first principle.

Although Field did not have much success in convincing his fellow justices of the validity of this reasoning, the theory that he launched was applied and honed in the high courts of several states. The most explicit expression of liberty of contract occurred in 1886, when the Pennsylvania Supreme Court struck down a law that required nothing more burdensome or obnoxious than that miners' wages be paid in cash rather than in goods or store orders. This regulation, the court ruled, was an invalid attempt by the legislature to prevent persons who were legally capable from making their own contracts. It would inhibit the rights of the employee as well as the employer, the court explained. "He may sell his labor for what he thinks best, whether money or goods, just as his employer may sell his iron or coal, and any and every law that proposes to prevent him from so doing is an infringement of his constitutional privileges, and is consequently vicious and void."

In the years that followed, the high courts of several states relied on liberty of contract to strike down a wide variety of laws regulating the conditions of employment. It provided the New York Court of Appeals with a legal theory for overruling the prohibition against making cigars in tenement houses. In Illinois the supreme court invalidated a requirement that certain businesses pay their employees on a weekly basis. Regulations that would limit the practice of paying employees in scrip that was redeemable at a company store were overruled in West Virginia and Illinois. Laws requiring that miners' pay be computed on the basis of the weight of coal before it was screened and prohibiting the practice of docking weavers' pay for imperfect work also fell under the judicial ax. State attempts to keep employers from discriminating against union workers by prohibiting "yellow dog contracts" met the same fate.

As might be expected, some lawyers and judges were not enamored of this new doctrine. One of its more sarcastic critics observed that "the spectacle of a government that cannot prohibit a contract merely because two grown persons desire to make it, is so utterly absurd as to be beyond the region of discussion if government of any kind is to continue." In reality there were all kinds of restrictions on what people could or could not agree to. There was no basis for liberty of contract in common law, much less in constitutional law. Besides, some critics believed that the statutes that were attacked in these cases did not involve contracts at all. They involved abuses—abuses that could only happen when there was such an inequality in bargaining power between the parties that any true agreement would be impossible.

Courts did not apply the liberty of contract doctrine in every case in which it was raised, and statutes that were attacked on that basis were not always invalidated. But those that were formed a substantial body of law. They provided ample authority upon which Weismann and Field would be able to build their case. What is more, there were a few cases that came close to being directly on point. In 1890 the California Supreme Court had invalidated a Los Angeles ordinance that provided an eight-hour day for workers on government projects. Within the next decade a general eight-hour ceiling in Nebraska, an Illinois law limiting the length of the workday for women in manufacturing, and an eight-hour day for Colorado miners were all overruled.

The problem facing Lochner's attorneys was that because these were all state court rulings, they would have only a limited impact on a case in the United States Supreme Court. The Supreme Court had recognized the doctrine of liberty of contract, but only once had it used the doctrine to invalidate a state law. That case, which involved a Louisiana prohibition on the sale of insurance policies issued by out-of-state companies, did not closely resemble the facts of Lochner's appeal.

The Court had claimed the right to review the substance of state legislation when it adopted the doctrine of substantive due process. It had stepped onto the legislative turf, but it was hesitant to press too hard. Rather, its tendency was to defer to the judgment of state legislatures. "Every possible presumption is in favor of the validity of a statute," wrote Justice John Harlan, "and this continues until the contrary is shown beyond a reasonable doubt." If all that can be said against a state law is that it is unwise or oppressive, then the proper appeal is not to the courts, Harlan explained, but to the legislature and the ballot box. A court cannot interfere without usurping the powers committed to another branch of government.

Although Harlan was most vocal in this respect, he was not alone. To be sure, instances in which the majority of the Court saw sufficient cause to overcome the presumption, or chose to ignore it altogether, could readily be found. The railroad rate cases *Reagan v. Farmers' Loan and Trust* and *Smyth v. Ames*, for example, were anything but displays of judicial deference to the legislative will. Yet this principle of presumed validity weighed heavily against the possibility that the Supreme Court would invalidate the New York Bakeshop Act. Most of the nine justices who would decide the case had at one time or another paid heed to it.

The prospects for Joseph Lochner looked grim indeed. In addition to the problem of overcoming this general presumption, his attorneys were faced with strong precedent against them. The Supreme Court had reviewed eight-hour workdays twice in the past, and on each occasion the statute had been upheld. Their only hope began with drawing some viable distinction between these two statutes and the New York ten-hour law.

The person charged with defending the ten-hour law was New York attorney general Julius M. Mayer. Mayer was a native of New York City and a graduate of Columbia Law School. Connections with the regular Republican organization early in his career helped to establish his private law practice. Between 1894 and 1898 he was retained as counsel for the city's excise board and building department. Like Weismann and Field, Mayer was part of the fusion campaign that elected Seth Low as mayor of New York City in 1901.

After the victory Mayer was appointed judge of the court of special sessions. Although his appointment was partly a concession to Boss Platt, Mayer appeared to have a cordial relationship with Low as well.

Mayer was still sitting on the New York City court when Lochner's appeal was filed. The case was started during the term of his predecessor and opponent for the attorney general post, John Cuneen. In the five months between the time the case went to the Supreme Court and his defeat in November 1904, however, Cuneen had done little to prepare a defense. Time had been lost for writing the state's legal brief and composing its oral argument, and in December the lame duck attorney general made the task even more urgent by agreeing with Weismann and Field to ask the Supreme Court to advance the case for an early hearing.

This in itself was not cause for panic. Much work would have to be done in a short time, but the law appeared to be on Mayer's side. The New York Court of Appeals, one of the leaders in overruling legislation on the basis of liberty of contract, had already upheld the statute. Besides, the attorney general had a strong place at which he could begin to build his defense of the ten-hour regulation. He needed simply to point to the two cases in which the United States Supreme Court had previously found shorter-hours laws to be constitutional. The first of these, and most closely in point, was *Holden v. Hardy*. It involved a Utah statute, passed in 1896, that placed an eight-hour ceiling on the workday of miners and workers in smelters and refineries. The majority opinion was written by Justice Henry Billings Brown, a Michigan jurist who had joined the Supreme Court in 1890.

By his own estimation, Brown was an extreme conservative. He was an admirer of Thomas M. Cooley and a friend and college classmate of fellow justice David Brewer. There can be little doubt that he favored the idea of liberty of contract and believed that the Court possessed extensive power to review the substance of state legislation. Yet in *Holden v. Hardy* Brown wrote an opinion upholding a statute that had been challenged on the basis of these very theories.

The reason slowly became evident in Brown's rambling opinion. "The right of contract," he wrote, "is itself subject to certain limitations which the State may lawfully impose in the exercise of its police powers." Because of an enormous increase in the number of occupations that were so dangerous to the health and safety of workers that they demanded special precautions, Brown explained, the police powers had greatly expanded during the preceding century. Mining was without a doubt one of those occupations; presumably smelting and refining were as well. Thus the decision to place a limit on the workday in these industries represented a legitimate exercise of the state's duty to preserve health and safety. The outcome of Brown's opinion had a ring of progressivism, but in truth all he had said was that the Utah statute fell within Stephen J. Field's limited definition of the police power.

Justice Brown did take notice of one of the major arguments made by proponents of eight-hour laws. Observing that employers and employees often do not negotiate from equal footing, he reasoned that when proprietors lay down the rules and laborers are practically constrained to obey them, self-interest is often an unsafe guide for determining what is detrimental to their health. Although this statement may have shed some light on Brown's personal sympathies, it was dictum and had absolutely no impact on the Court's ruling. *Holden v. Hardy* said nothing with respect to shorter-hours laws in general. The majority had agreed that laws limiting the hours of labor in unsafe or unhealthy occupations were constitutional, nothing more. And two of the justices even dissented from that outcome.

One of the dissenters was Brown's Yale classmate David Josiah Brewer. Brewer, the nephew of Stephen J. Field, appeared to have inherited the role of the Court's leading champion of the negative state. In fact, he may have been even more outspoken than his colorful uncle. "The paternal theory of government is to me odious," he once announced in a dissenting opinion. "The utmost possible liberty to the individual, and the fullest possible protection to him and his property, is both the limitation and duty of government." Without this, he predicted, "*Looking Backward* is nearer than a dream." In *Holden v. Hardy* Brewer chose not to state why he disagreed with the majority. Instead he joined with Rufus W. Peckham in dissenting without writing an opinion.

About five and a half years later, in the case of *Atkin v. Kansas*, the Court upheld another eight-hour statute. This case involved an eight-hour limit on the workday for government employees and for employees of contractors who were working on public projects. The opinion of the majority was written by John Harlan; as might be expected, he emphasized that a presumption should exist in favor of the validity of the statute. "Legislative enactments should be recognized and enforced by the courts as embodying the will of the people," Harlan wrote, "unless they are plainly and palpably, beyond all question, in violation of the fundamental law of the Constitution."

Even though the parties had stipulated that the occupations that were controlled by the Kansas statute were not dangerous, the *Atkin* case still did not represent an expansion of the decision in *Holden v. Hardy*. The impact of this case was limited because the law applied only to government projects. The state, which was in effect a party to the contract, had a right to control the conditions of employment for work done on its behalf. Whether a similar limitation on the workday of laborers in purely private work would be constitutional was, in Harlan's words, "a question of very large import, which we have no occasion now to determine or even consider."

Atkin v. Kansas was significant for another reason, however. A third justice joined the ranks of the dissenters. Justice Brewer was seldom inclined to pay deference to legislative judgment when it came to economic regulation. "The police power," he once chided, "is the refuge for timid judges to escape the obligation of denouncing a wrong in a case where some supposed general or public good is the object of legislation." He could be counted upon to dissent once again. This time, however, Brewer was joined not only by Peckham but also by Chief Justice Melville Weston Fuller. Two justices from the majority had resigned since *Holden v. Hardy*. But the two who replaced them, Oliver Wendell Holmes and William Rufus Day, voted to uphold the statute in Atkin.

If Lochner's attorneys were counting votes, it seemed obvious that they could depend upon only Brewer, Peckham, and Fuller to support their attack on the Bakeshop Act's ten-hour workday. Based upon past performance alone, it appeared as though they would lose by a vote of 6 to 3. But *Holden v. Hardy* and *Atkin v. Kansas* did more than provide a count. These cases also gave the competing sides their cues.

Weismann and Frank Harvey Field took theirs and played the part as expected. In their written brief, they argued that the Bakeshop Act violated the liberty of contract of both bakeshop workers and employers. This, however, was not enough to win their case. No court had ever held that liberty of contract was absolute. It protected individuals from governmental intrusion that went beyond a state's proper authority, but it had to give way to a legitimate exercise of the police power of the states. Lochner's attorneys seemed well aware that their case hinged on the Court adopting the narrow definition of the police power.

With this in mind they distanced themselves from *Holden v. Hardy* by claiming that baking was not a hazardous occupation. The ten-hour workday was not passed for the purpose of protecting the health of bakers or the public, they said. Therefore it was not a proper exercise of state authority but merely a labor law. It was on this point that the appearance of Henry Weismann in oral argument may have had some impact. Who would better know the purpose of the law than a person who, as a labor leader, had participated in the fight to have it passed?

The attorney general was not quite so alert. He argued, as he should have, that the Court should defer to the judgment of the New York legislature on this matter and that the burden fell on his opponents to prove that the Bakeshop Act was not a legitimate exercise of the police power. He also properly argued that the shorter-hours provision was passed as part of an effort to protect the health of both bakers and the public. But Mayer ignored the possibility that he might lose on this final point.

Mining and even smelting were generally thought to be dangerous occupations. It was a relatively simple matter to get the Court to take judicial notice of that fact when it was reviewing the Utah eight-hour law, but it was going to be much harder to convince it that baking was hazardous as well. There was nothing dramatic about a baker's death—no cave-ins, molten metal, or bone-crushing machinery. The only hazard that was thought to exist came in the form of a lingering and slowly debilitating lung disease. In a way, Attorney General Mayer's case had an image problem—an image problem that was revealed by Judge Bartlett, of the New York Court of Appeals, who surmised that the claim that baking is unhealthy "will surprise the bakers and good housewives of this state."

The existence of such skepticism should have had an impact on the attorney general's tactics. In the first place, it should have been obvious that emphasis on scientific or quantitative evidence showing that baking was an unhealthy business would be invaluable. Judge Vann had done this in his concurring opinion in the New York court. It would have been easy to emphasize and expand upon his sources. Instead Mayer was content in writing one sentence, in which he merely directed the Court to that earlier opinion.

It also would have been wise to prepare a fallback position—that is, to argue that even if the Court chose to believe that the ten-hour limitation on the bakers' workday was not a health measure, it was nevertheless a legitimate exercise of New York's police power. Yet even though the authors of the two earlier cases dealing with workday limitations had hinted that this question needed to be addressed, Mayer ignored it. Conflict between differing views on the extent of the police power was likely to be the center point of some case, and there were reasons to believe that it just might be this one.

Only a little more than one year had passed since Justice Harlan had provided a clue as to the direction that the attorney general's argument might take. In the *Atkin* case he observed that the state of Kansas "may have intended to give sanction to the view, held by many, that, all things considered, the general welfare of employees, mechanics and workmen . . . will be subserved if labor for eight hours was taken to be a full day's work." He further suggested that it may have been motivated by the belief that "the restriction of a day's work to that number of hours would promote morality, improve the physical and intellectual condition of laborers and workmen and enable them to better discharge the duties appertaining to citizenship." Harlan did not say whether he thought that this was an adequate justification for the legislation; but the broader definition of the police power and some of the rationale used by supporters of the eight-hour movement could be found in his words.

Although the Kansas eight-hour law was upheld on narrower grounds, there were Supreme Court cases that Mayer could have used to support the contention that the state's police power was not limited to protecting public health, safety, and morals. State laws prohibiting the practice of medicine without a license, regulating the grades of coal oil sold to the public, and regulating the sale of oleomargarine all had been upheld by the Court. Public health and safety was possibly a concern in these cases, but in each instance the state was also motivated by a desire to enhance the public welfare by protecting its citizens against fraud. Prevention of fraud was the more obvious concern in two later cases, in which state prohibitions on the sale of stocks and commodities on margin were held constitutional. And an even broader conception of the public interest came into play when the Court verified the constitutionality of a statute that required that railroads pay dismissed employees the wages they had already earned.

Add to these the numerous state cases that upheld regulations of the relationship between employer and employee, and it is undeniable that there was plenty for Mayer to work with. Yet in an incredibly sketchy eighteen-page brief, the attorney general virtually conceded that a state law that could not be classified as promoting the health, safety, or morals of the public was not a legitimate exercise of the police power.

There is no way of knowing why the attorney general offered such an abbreviated written argument. It could have been a matter of overconfidence, or he could have seen some tactical advantage in being silent with respect to the definition of the police power. It is also possible, however, that Julius Mayer simply lacked enthusiasm for the case. Examples of attorneys general presenting weak cases in defense of reform statutes could be found in the recent past. In *Holden v. Hardy* the attorney general of Utah had absolutely refused to defend his state's eight-hour statute. The defense was eventually prepared by the American Federation of Labor, which hired a private lawyer for the case. In a similar vein, Richard Olney, the U.S. attorney general who lost the *Sugar Trust* case, took pride in not prosecuting cases under the Sherman Antitrust Act. Like public officials before him, the New York attorney general may have found himself charged with defending a law to which he was philosophically opposed.

Cause for this suspicion could be found in Mayer's later career. His political leanings were hard to identify in his early years, when he had ties with Boss Platt but also supported reformer Seth Low and had a good relationship with Theodore Roosevelt. As time passed, however, it became evident that Mayer was more closely aligned to the conservative wing of the Republican party. In 1912, with the backing of President Taft's personal secretary, Charles D. Hilles, Mayer was appointed to the United States District Court. The appointment was vigorously opposed by reformer Florence Kelly, who charged that

Mayer used his influence as president of a Jewish children's protective society to oppose a proposed child labor law. In 1921 his promotion to the United States Court of Appeals was delayed while supporters countered charges that he was "a friend of the interests."

There was, however, another plausible explanation for Mayer's somewhat halfhearted effort. Less than two months after the *Lochner* case was argued, and coincidentally on the same day that the Court announced its decision, he was scheduled to appear in another case before the Supreme Court—one that was far more sensational and far more important to his political career. It would determine the validity of the state's franchise tax on streetcar lines, tunnels, gasworks, and other public utilities.

For years corporations owning these franchises were able to avoid being taxed on their value. But in 1899 with a great deal of fanfare and a hard push from Governor Theodore Roosevelt, the state enacted a special franchise tax law. Now the legality of that law was being tested in a series of fourteen connected cases. Aligned against the attorney general were some of the most powerful lawyers in the state. William D. Guthrie and Elihu Root represented various street railways, and Root was joined by Boss Platt's son, Frank H. Platt, in representing several gas companies. The combined cases took several days of oral argument and produced hundreds of pages of legal briefs.

Although Mayer retained a well-known attorney, Louis Marshall, to help prepare the state's case, it may well be that the newly elected attorney general was simply overwhelmed. Oral argument in the *Lochner* case was scheduled for February 23; the *Franchise Tax Cases*, which were argued on April 17, had originally been scheduled for oral argument even earlier. Within five months from the time he took office, Mayer had to prepare and argue two cases before the nation's highest court. There is no question which of the two was more important to him—*Lochner* was not even mentioned in his official report for 1905. The state's work on the *Franchise Tax Cases* was much more impressive, and in a speech one year later, Mayer boasted that victory in the *Franchise Tax Cases* had allowed the state to levy taxes on four hundred million dollars' worth of property. Thus defense of the New York Bakeshop Act may have been slighted in the rush to prepare for another case that the attorney general ranked as a higher priority.

CHAPTER 9

The Final Forum

When Henry Weisman, Frank Harvey Field, and Julius Mayer gathered for the reading of the Court's decision on April 17, 1905, it is unlikely that any of them felt very confident about the outcome. By tradition, a justice who had voted with the majority was chosen to write the opinion of the Court and would announce it in open court. Henry Weismann's pulse must have quickened when he saw who that justice was going to be for the case of *Lochner v. New York*. Rufus W. Peckham, possibly the Court's most consistent advocate of the negative state, had been chosen to represent the majority.

Although he was not quite as outspoken as Brewer, Peckham had made his views on the extent of the police power well known. Sitting as a judge on the New York Court of Appeals, he once described a law that regulated grain elevator rates as being "vicious in its nature and communistic in its tendency." Peckham came to the Supreme Court in 1895 with a reputation for reversing the decisions of lower courts. In the ten years that had passed, he usually had sided with Brewer in promoting the laissez-faire interpretation of the Constitution. Both men had dissented from the earlier decisions that upheld shorter-hours laws. Before a word was even spoken, the attorneys who sat in the courtroom awaiting the decision must have known what the outcome was going to be.

Justice Peckham did not disappoint his listeners. The New York Bakeshop Act, he declared, "necessarily interferes with the right of contract between the employer and employees, concerning the number of hours which the latter may labor in the bakery of the employer." The right of contract—in this case the right to purchase and sell labor—is part of the liberty protected by the Fourteenth Amendment, Peckham continued, "unless there are circumstances which exclude that right." He could find no such circumstances.

The only circumstance that would have satisfied him was proof that the law was enacted to protect the health of bakeshop workers. Otherwise, he said, it was not a reasonable and appropriate exercise of the state's police power, but merely an arbitrary interference with the right of a worker to sell his labor in a manner that might seem to him appropriate or necessary for the support of himself and his family. Given this emphasis of his concern for the laborer, it is not surprising that Peckham decided there was no reasonable foundation for holding that the Bakeshop Act was necessary to safeguard the public health or the health of individuals in the baking trade. His conclusion was not reached through any obvious effort to weigh available evidence, however. In its place Peckham invoked the time-honored practice of "taking judicial notice" by observing that "to the common understanding the trade of baking has never been regarded as an unhealthy one."

The *Lochner* case afforded Peckham an opportunity to express disdain for what he perceived to be a trend toward paternalistic legislation. "It is impossible for us to shut our eyes to the fact that many laws of this character, while passed under what is claimed to be the police power for the purpose of protecting the public health or welfare, are, in reality, passed for other motives," he explained. Peckham did not explain what improper motives he had in mind, but he proclaimed that the state had to show more than a vague link to health and safety. Otherwise any type of regulation would be possible. Directing attention to the extremes, he projected that the work hours not only of employees but also of employers might be limited. Artisans, scientists, doctors, and even lawyers could be forbidden to fatigue their brains and bodies by prolonged hours of exercise. The rights of all individuals to do what they want with the fruit of their labor would be at the mercy of legislative majorities.

"This is not a question of substituting the judgment of the Court for that of the legislature," Peckham explained. But of course that is exactly what he was doing. The Bakeshop Act had been passed not once, but twice, by the legislature of the state of New York. Both times the vote had been unanimous, and amendments to the ten-hour workday provision were specifically at issue in the second vote. At the very least it could be said that one hundred nineteen legislators had voted in favor of the ten-hour ceiling.

Although some studies indicated that the trade was not unusually dangerous, there was ample statistical support for the contention that baking was an unhealthy occupation. A study conducted by the state labor commissioner one year before the Bakeshop Act was passed had reached that conclusion, and it was supported by a substantial portion of the scientific and medical opinion of the time. Attorney General Mayer had not emphasized this in his brief, but Judge Vann had done so in a concurring opinion that was available to the justices as part of the record of the case.

All of the justices who heard Joseph Lochner's appeal had been sitting on the Court two years earlier when, in *Atkin v. Kansas*, they ruled that legislative enactments should be recognized and enforced "unless they are plainly and palpably, beyond all question, in violation of the fundamental law of the Constitution." According to that standard, when the validity of a statute was being questioned, the burden of proof fell upon those who asserted that it was unconstitutional. John Harlan, who wrote Atkin for a 6 to 3 majority, argued this point often and vehemently. For him, that there was room for debate and for an honest difference of opinion should have put an end to the case. Even if a statute seemed unwise or unjust, Harlan believed the responsibility for making that determination belonged to the legislature.

If the Court had remained true to this part of the *Atkin* decision, the New York Bakeshop Act would have been upheld. But Peckham shifted the burden. Taking a weight from the shoulders of Weismann and Field, he presented the attorney general, the legislature, or anyone else who might want to defend the statute with a duty to clearly demonstrate that there was some fair ground to say that the public health or the health of bakers would suffer if the hours of labor were not shortened.

The vote was close—so close that historical rumor has it that the case was at first decided the other way and that Harlan initially prepared a draft that was to be the opinion of the Court. Nevertheless when the final vote was taken, a 5 to 4 majority of the Court agreed that the ten-hour limitation on the workday of New York bakers was unconstitutional. At some point Harlan had lost two votes. Justices Henry Billings Brown and Joseph McKenna, who had stood with him in *Atkin*, switched. Gone with their votes was the principle that an act of a state legislature was presumed to be valid.

Gone too was any doubt about how the Court intended to define the police power in cases involving state "experimentation" with labor regulations. "There is no contention that bakers as a class are not equal in intelligence and capacity to men in other trades or manual occupations, or that they are not able to assert their rights and care for themselves without the protecting arm of the state," wrote Peckham. The term "public welfare" appeared in Peckham's text, but the majority plainly had agreed that the only valid justification for such legislation was its relationship to health and safety. Six years after Justice Stephen J. Field's death, the Court had finally adopted his view of a limited police power.

Regardless of its original purpose, Harlan's draft now represented a minority view that would appear in case reports as an addendum to the opinion of the Court. Oliver Wendell Holmes added his own written dissent as well. Each dissent attacked the majority on different grounds, and each dissent provides valuable insight into the significance of the *Lochner* case.

———

Standing six feet two inches tall, clean-shaven, and square jawed, John Marshall Harlan cut an imposing figure. His wife recalled that when she first saw him, "he walked as if the whole world belonged to him." From what others have since written, it appears that she had sized up her future husband with uncanny accuracy. Born in 1833 to a wealthy Kentucky family, Harlan was raised in a mansion staffed by slaves. His father, a successful and politically active lawyer, had been state attorney general and a member of the U.S. House of Representatives. Naturally, Harlan was exposed to politics from an early age. He matured in the years immediately preceding the Civil War, a confusing and trying time in American history, especially in the border state of Kentucky.

From his father, Harlan inherited a belief in a strong Union. But he was also convinced that slaves were property and that government should not interfere with the rights of slaveholders. As the nation approached civil war it became increasingly apparent that these two positions were in serious conflict. Yet Harlan maintained them both throughout the war, fighting with distinction on the side of the Union and fervently preaching against emancipation.

He continued to speak in the same vein after the war. When the Thirteenth Amendment was passed by Congress and sent to the states for ratification, Harlan labeled it a flagrant violation of states' rights and an example of tyranny of the majority in taking property away from slaveholders. After the amendment was ratified, he opposed the Civil Rights Act of 1866 and the Fourteenth Amendment—keys to Radical Republican hopes of ensuring "freedmen" the rights of citizenship.

Harlan lost on all counts in those early battles over reconstruction. Within two years, however, he reversed position, joining the ranks of his former foes and defending Republican policies. His conversion became obvious in 1871 when, running as the Republican candidate for governor of Kentucky, he could be found courting the votes of former slaves. His opponent in that race made the most of it, calling Harlan "a weathercock who turned whichever way the political wind blew."

Whatever the reason, shifts in position mark Harlan's career on the Court as well as in politics. Those who try to find consistency in his judicial opinions always seem to encounter glaring exceptions. It could be that Harlan was simply opportunistic. With respect to slavery, however, subsequent events make that hard to believe. Thirty-seven years after his acceptance of the Republican party and its plan for reconstruction, Harlan was the lone dissenter in *Plessy v. Ferguson*, the case that established the separate-but-equal doctrine. "The white race deems itself the dominant race in this country," he wrote in dissent. "But in view of the Constitution, in the eye of the law, there is in this country no dominant ruling class of citizens. There is no caste here. Our Constitution is color-blind." This became the most famous statement of his long tenure on the bench, and given his insulated position, it was hardly the language of a man who had merely blown with the political wind.

It is possible that he was simply open-minded. One of his biographers points out that although Harlan had harangued against foreigners and Catholics when campaigning for the Know-Nothing party in 1856, he changed his mind after observing the bravery of Irish and German troops during the war. It is just as likely, however, that this apparent inconsistency was the product of a distinctive personal philosophy. If so, it is one that has continually perplexed everyone except

Harlan himself. The only conspicuous consistency running throughout his writings is a deep religious conviction and a strong faith in the Constitution. Observing these traits, one of his fellow justices joked that the Kentuckian went to bed "with one hand on the Constitution and the other on the Bible, safe and happy in a perfect faith in justice and righteousness."

John Marshall Harlan was not a hesitant man. He may have changed his stance, but when he decided on a direction he was not afraid to speak his piece. Once he took a position, he took it forcefully. His attitude in this respect was illustrated during his campaign for governor of Kentucky. To detractors who charged him with being a weathercock he responded, "Let it be said that I am right rather than consistent."

By the time *Lochner v. New York* was argued, Harlan had been on the Court for twenty-six years. He was probably best known for his stinging dissents. One year before *Plessy*, Harlan wrote a well-known dissent to the Court's invalidation of the graduated income tax. He accused the majority of declaring that the U.S. government had been so formed that in matters of taxation it offered privileges to landowners and investors that were not available to those whose income was derived from the labor of their hands, skills, or brains. Taking to task those who argued that the tax was an assault upon capital, he argued that the duty to "stand in the breech for the protection of just rights of property against the advancing hosts of Socialism" rests in the Congress, not the Court.

In a dissent to *Hurtado v. California*, Harlan became the first justice to enunciate the "incorporation doctrine." This theory, which eventually became important in modern civil liberties cases, holds that the first eight amendments of the Bill of Rights apply directly to the states through the Fourteenth Amendment guarantee that no citizen may be deprived of life, liberty, or property without due process of law.

A half century later, recalling some of these dissents, many liberals were inclined to view Harlan as a prophet and hero. Indeed, his viewpoints may have been precursors of many modern opinions regarding civil rights and civil liberties. When attention is turned to economic and social regulation and reform, however, his position is not so easily categorized. He argued for a federal income tax, a strict interpretation of antitrust laws, and a strong interstate commerce commission. But his attachment to the principles of laissez faire and individualism was strong enough to lead fellow justice Henry Billings Brown to observe that he was especially solicitous that the property of the citizen should be protected against state laws that under the guise of regulation rendered it valueless.

As the nineteenth century came to an end, the Supreme Court firmly cemented its authority to review state regulatory legislation. The case that is often said to have signaled that development was *Smyth v. Ames.* It was written by John Harlan, who declared that "the perpetuity of our institutions and the liberty which is enjoyed under them depend, in no small degree, upon the power given to the judiciary to declare null and void all legislation that is clearly repugnant to the supreme law of the land."

Smyth v. Ames demonstrated not only that Harlan recognized the Court's authority to invalidate regulatory statutes but also that he was willing to use it. Yet he often warned his colleagues to use it sparingly—to avoid "judicial legislation." This was the thrust of his opinion in the *Atkin* case, which upheld a Kansas eight-hour law. It would also be the crux of his dissent in *Lochner v. New York.* The *Lochner* majority, Harlan said, "expanded the scope of the Fourteenth Amendment far beyond the original purpose, and brought under the supervision of the Court matters which belonged exclusively to the legislative departments of the states." But in what sense had the Court entered the domain of legislation?

"What is the true ground for the state to take between legitimate protection, by legislation, of the public health and liberty of contract," he observed, "is not a question easily solved." Having first noted the existence of scientific authority in support of the belief that baking was an unhealthy profession, he reminded his fellow justices that there were many reasons also supporting the theory that "more than ten hours of steady work each day, from week to week, in a bakery or confectionery establishment, may endanger the health or shorten the lives of the workmen." Given that such reasons existed, he continued, "that ought to be the end of this case." State legislative actions should not be invalidated unless they are "plainly, palpably, beyond all question, inconsistent with the Constitution."

The language of this dissent was strong. Yet on careful reading, it is plain that Harlan was simply attacking the majority on their own terms. They had been wrong in applying the doctrine of liberty of contract to invalidate this state law in this case, but not because they had misinterpreted the doctrine or erroneously defined the police power. Harlan had in fact joined the majority in accepting Stephen Field's limited definition of the police power. His dissent rested on the position that "health and safety" provided the only legitimate justification for the state to pass such a law. But unlike Peckham and the majority, in light of the evidence he was willing to presume that this had been the motivation guiding the New York State Assembly.

———

"The Fourteenth Amendment does not enact Mr. Herbert Spencer's *Social Statics*." With this one sentence, explained his friend Harold Laski, Justice Holmes exposed the inarticulate major premise of the *Lochner* majority. His terse two-page dissent elucidated reformers' misgivings about the decision and more. Oliver Wendell Holmes Jr. had been sitting on the Supreme Court for less than two years when *Lochner* was decided, but he was hardly an unknown. He had been a justice of the Massachusetts Supreme Court for twenty years when Theodore Roosevelt nominated him for the nation's highest court in 1902. By then Holmes had long established his reputation as a legal scholar. Early in his career as a practicing lawyer he edited the prestigious *American Law Review*, and in 1881 he wrote a classic legal treatise entitled *The Common Law*. One year later a new chair was established for him at Harvard Law School, where he taught for a year before assuming his position on the Massachusetts high court.

Born in 1841 into a family that was part of the "Brahmin caste" of New England, Holmes's circumstances were marked by pedigree and privilege. But this elite class of New Englanders prided itself on intellectual prowess as well, and in the late nineteenth century it was experiencing a renaissance. Holmes's father, a well-known physician and author, was associated with a literary group called the Saturday Club. Its members included Ralph Waldo Emerson, Henry Wadsworth Longfellow, Richard Henry Dana, and Harvard professors Louis Agassiz, James Russell Lowell, and Benjamin Peirce. As a youth, Holmes had the opportunity to associate with these great thinkers of his time, and he was even close to some. Emerson, for example, critiqued a youthful essay on Plato, and Holmes sought his advice before embarking on a career in law.

Throughout his life Holmes formed and maintained friendships with people of intellectual distinction. In the field of American law, Felix Frankfurter, Louis Brandeis, Roscoe Pound, and Learned Hand come to mind. Outside of the profession, Henry Adams, William and Henry James, and A. G. Segwick are some that might be remembered today. The point is that Holmes's proclivities were toward the historical, literary, and philosophical disciplines; and these carried over to his legal writings and judicial opinions, which at times bore the stamp of an essayist and philosopher.

This may explain in part why no justice of the Supreme Court has attracted more attention or been the subject of more comment with more fervor than has Holmes. Over time he has become as much legend as judge. And as is often the case with legendary figures, those who study him are not in agreement about the value of his contribution, nor for that matter about just what his philosophy entailed. Various commentators have placed Holmes into widely disparate categories—positivist, cynic, social Darwinist, liberal, legal realist, relativist. Such attempts to categorize and even to assess the long-term impact of the justice's career lend themselves to dispute. But certain aspects of Holmes's thinking are unmistakable.

Interestingly, Holmes had little sympathy for reform. He never expressed a systematic theory of economics, but he did lean toward the classic doctrines of nineteenth-century laissez faire. Harold Laski recalled that "the basis of Holmes' economic faith would have been rejected neither by Adam Smith nor Ricardo." Private ownership and self-interest made up its foundation, and he distrusted what he deemed to be the futile if not mischievous economic tinkering of welfare legislation.

Although he did not join reformers in rejecting laissez-faire economics, Holmes was plainly with them and with Roscoe Pound in disliking the legal method of reasoning that deduced conclusions from a priori principles. In an 1897 speech presented at Boston University School of Law, Holmes argued that the legal method suffered from a "fallacy of logical form." It perceived the universe in terms of a fixed quantitative relation between every phenomenon and its antecedents and consequences, he continued. Thus it operated from the notion that a legal system could be worked out like mathematics from general axioms of conduct. This mode of thinking was entirely natural for lawyers, in part because of their training, but also because "it flatters a longing for certainty." But certainty, he warned, is an illusion. "No concrete proposition is self evident, no matter how ready we may be to accept it." Reflected in this conclusion was the nucleus of Holmes's thinking—his well-known skepticism. "When I say that a thing is true I mean that I can't help believing it—and nothing more," he explained. "But as I observe that the cosmos is not always limited by my 'can't helps' I don't bother about absolute truth or even inquire whether there is such a thing, but define the truth as the system of my limitations."

The uncertainty reflected in Holmes's description of his "can't helps" should not be confused with timidity. Observing that Holmes was the least hesitant of men, one of his critics, Yosal Rogat, later noted that it was difficult to think of anyone who expressed fewer qualifications or occupied fewer halfway positions. What then did this skepticism mean? Rogat thought that it could be translated into crude relativism: might makes right. He argued that Holmes was too detached from the consequences of his decisions and too fatalistic in his attitude toward power. Rogat's argument seems convincing, but it fails to recognize that one can act on a belief without insisting that it is universal or immutable law.

Holmes did not distrust his own principles or beliefs. Rather, he distrusted dogma. If the search for truth was subject to ever-changing human limitations and personal prejudices, as he believed, the best approximation of truth would be reached through the free play of ideas. The meaning of all this has been the subject of considerable debate. What is important, however, is that Holmes's uncertainty, his "can't helps," his skepticism ultimately boil down to a suspicion of first principles. Principles elevated to a level of immutable law posed the greatest danger to a free exchange of ideas. Holmes believed that rather than providing truth, they limited the search for the truth.

Skepticism carried over into Holmes's ideas about the role of judges. In 1913 he told a Harvard Law School audience that "all law embodies beliefs that have triumphed in the battle of ideas and then have translated themselves into action." So long as there is still doubt and opposite convictions continue to battle, he said, "it is a mistake if a judge reads his conscious or unconscious sympathy with one side or the other prematurely into law, and forgets that what seems to him to be first principles are believed by half of his fellow men to be wrong."

The impact his beliefs would have on his opinions from the bench of the United States Supreme Court was made clear in his first written opinion. "Considerable latitude must be allowed for differences of view," he wrote in *Otis v. Parker*. "Otherwise a constitution, instead of embodying only relatively fundamental rules of right, as generally understood by all English-speaking communities, would become the partisan of a particular set of ethical or economical opinions which by no means are held *semper ubique et ab omnibus*."

It is popular today to speak of the Supreme Court as the "forum of principle." Principle, as distinguished from policy, is said to be "a standard observed, not because it will advance or secure an economic, political, or social situation deemed desirable, but because it is a requirement of justice or fairness or some other dimension of morality." Because it is appointed, life tenured, and thus insulated from the pressures of politics, the federal judiciary is thought to be the institution best suited to determine such matters of principle. Michael J. Perry, for example, maintains that "the Court is ordained by tradition to serve as the forum for the subtle dialectical interplay of complex, principled ethical discourse." He and others believe that of the branches of government, the politically insulated Court is the most likely to shed the sediment of old moralities and move toward moral evolution. At the very least, judicial review is said to encourage and increase dialogue and thereby move us more certainly in the direction of truth.

Modern scholars have not forgotten the *Lochner* case, but their memory of it has been selective. The decision has come to be known as an instance of the Court mistakenly dabbling in matters of economic policy. When the background of the case is recalled, however, it is readily apparent that it involved something more: it was a dispute between competing principles. Holmes recognized this and pointed out the implications in his short dissent. "A constitution is not intended to embody a particular economic theory," he wrote. "It is made for people of fundamentally differing views, and the accident of our finding certain opinions natural and familiar or novel or even shocking ought not to conclude our judgment upon the question whether statutes embodying them conflict with the Constitution of the United States."

Several years later, Learned Hand wondered why the validity of the bakeshop law ever became a matter of health in the first place. His answer was predictable. The crucial aspect of *Lochner* was that the majority had finally adopted Field's definition of the police power. It had embraced a laissez-faire–social Darwinian interpretation of the Constitution. This did not mean that a complete absence of state involvement in the economy was assured. Some regulation might be acceptable under this interpretation, but only so long as it fit within the laissez-faire framework.

The word "interpretation" should be emphasized. Laissez faire–social Darwinism is not part of the Constitution of the United States. The Court took two large steps away from that document to reach the conclusion that states were confined to that framework in managing their internal affairs. Initially mutation of the Fourteenth Amendment's due process guarantee provided the means by which the Court was able to review the substance of laws dealing with a state's management of its internal affairs. Then liberty of contract provided an extra constitutional theory upon which the laissez-faire boundary was erected around a state's police power.

Almost anywhere else Rufus Peckham could have spoken his mind with little harm done. But the American system of government tends to give the Supreme Court the final word on what is and what is not constitutional. Its decisions therefore often represent much more than a final determination in a specific dispute between competing parties. They become part of the nation's fundamental law. As such they carry an air of immutability, of being first principles upon which all other laws should be based. This was the implication of the *Lochner* decision that most concerned Justice Holmes.

———

Both dissenters to the *Lochner* decision would have preferred that the Court start from a presumption that the legislature's act was valid. But they preferred this approach for entirely different reasons. Harlan expressed the presumption in this way: "The state is not amendable to the judiciary in respect of its legislative enactments, unless such enactments are plainly, palpably, beyond all question, inconsistent with the Constitution of the United States." Inconsistent according to whom? Harlan's test was entirely subjective, leaving the decision to the whim of the Court. He was in essence saying, We the Court define the Constitution. We determine the principles upon which legislation should be drafted. But if the judiciary is to perform its function, it must be generous in allowing the legislatures to apply those principles. Where questions of detail exist, the legislature should be given the benefit of the doubt.

Holmes strived for a more objective test and at least created one more stringent than Harlan's. The meaning of the Fourteenth Amendment would be perverted, he wrote, "unless it can be said that a rational and fair man necessarily would admit that the statute proposed would infringe fundamental principles as they have been understood by the traditions of our people and our law." Even under this test the ultimate decision would of course still lie with the Court. If Holmes was seeking complete objectivity, he failed. Objectivity, however, was not the only thing that set his "rational man" test apart from Harlan's search for "plain and palpable" inconsistency with the Constitution.

In Holmes's view, the Court's function was that of a sentry rather than a navigator. His test—that no statute should be declared unconstitutional unless a rational person would necessarily admit that it would infringe upon fundamental principles as understood by American laws and traditions—created a greater burden and carried a different emphasis than that offered by Harlan. Under it the legislature has as much right to make determinations of principle as does the Court. Holmes had stated this even more plainly in a decision for the Court one year earlier: "Great constitutional provisions must be administered with caution. Some play must be allowed for the points of the machine, and it must be remembered that legislatures are ultimate guardians of the liberties and welfare of the people in quite as great a degree as the courts."

Each dissenter was advocating a form of judicial restraint, and their proposed tests for constitutionality reflected how their notions of restraint differed. For John Harlan, the Supreme Court's function involved a search for absolutes. He fully knew what they were and where they came from, even if others might not be able to discern the pattern of his thought. Harlan's idea of restraint was for the Court to avoid becoming burdened with the details of applying the first principles it had enunciated. In Oliver Wendell Holmes's eyes, judicial restraint was something quite different. His idea of the Court's function was an extension of his skepticism and avoidance of absolutes. Holmes's dissent in *Lochner* displayed his reluctance to discover new first principles in the guise of interpretation.

The symbolic importance of *Lochner v. New York* is beyond question. For more than thirty years it served reformers as evidence of the conservative nature of the judiciary and as a striking example of its usurpation of political power. Even today this historical period marked by judicial interference with reform is referred to as "the *Lochner* Era," and the terms "lochnerism" and "lochnerian" can be found in legal writings. The Holmes dissent added fuel to this legacy, but it also explained how the timeless significance of the decision goes beyond symbolism. Holmes recognized that the Court's impact on the public conscience in defining the parameters of moral and philosophical debate, although intangible, was very real. To understand this is to understand why a case so trivial in terms of its direct result has become such an important part of constitutional history.

CHAPTER 10

Reform's Nemesis

Henry Weismann never again argued a case before a New York or federal appellate court. The Supreme Court's decision in *Lochner v. New York* may have been a nova in his legal career, but as a practical matter it was not a brilliant event. He and Frank Harvey Field had literally done no more than to save Joseph Lochner the expense of paying a fifty-dollar fine. Yet thirty to forty years later, when the Supreme Court blocked much of Franklin D. Roosevelt's New Deal legislation, the name of this obscure bakeshop owner could induce extreme displeasure and exasperation with the judicial branch of American government. Even now Lochner's name has a significant impact among those who study the Supreme Court. *Lochner v. New York* is commonly recognized as one of the most important, or at least most controversial, cases in constitutional history.

Given this current stature, it is interesting that initial public reaction to the Court's ruling was very subdued. If newspaper reports are any indication, no one other than the parties and attorneys involved was excitedly anticipating the pending decision. Only one major newspaper in the state of New York followed the case as it progressed through the courts, and it did so in a rather matter-of-fact manner. The press did report the Supreme Court's decision. It reached the front page of the *New York Times* and the *New York Tribune.* They and other state papers carried stories on the future of labor laws, labor's reaction, and Henry Weismann's role; but reports on the case were dispassionate. They conveyed no sense of victory or foreboding, no predictions of doom or salvation. Outside of the state, reports on the case were sometimes buried in the middle of the paper. One newspaper that did print an editorial was the *New York Press.* Surprisingly, the *Press,* which had influenced enactment of the Bakeshop Act by carrying Edward Marshall's exposé of the baking industry, now expressed mild satisfaction with the Court's decision.

Reaction in the labor press was, as should have been expected, negative. Headlines in the *New York Evening Journal* depicted the decision as "A Sad Day for Labor Legislation." In the article that followed, the *Evening Journal* reported that Justice Peckham and Counsel Weismann "appeared to be suffering from a malignant attack of Fourteenth Amendmentitus." Noting that Peckham's opinion had been "very solicitous of the rights of the workingman," it went on to ridicule the "kind-hearted justice" for having presumed too much. Nobody, it explained, had heard the journeyman bakers objecting to the ten-hour law.

The *Evening Journal's* editorial was accurate in at least one respect—journeyman bakers did not express the least bit of gratitude for the liberty that the Supreme Court had granted to them. This was made very clear in a two-part report on the decision published in the *Bakers' Journal*. This report by the voice of the journeyman bakers' union was actually a reprint of an article written by socialist attorney Morris Hillquit. The decision in *Lochner v. New York* meant that "it is unconstitutional if legislation provides and takes care of the interests of workingmen," he complained. "It is unconstitutional if bakery workers demand eight hours and day work; it is unconstitutional if they ask for a humane existence; if they begin to know their human rights; or demand to be treated like men." Hillquit summed up the decision in the same manner as he had explained it: "Everything that furthers the interest of employers is constitutional," while everything "which may be undertaken for the welfare of the working people and aims for the emancipation of the proletariat" is unconstitutional.

Defiance complemented this biting sarcasm as union leaders threatened to strike in protest of the Court's decision. "We do not consider the decision of the United States Supreme Court a victory for the boss bakers, for the simple reason that the regulation of working hours in bakeshops is not a matter of court decisions but a matter to be settled by workers only," they declared. "The question—as we look upon it—is not whether the Supreme Court declared the 10 hour law constitutional, but whether the bakery workers are willing to work longer than 10 hours per day or 60 hours per week." Despite all this rhetoric, no tangible backlash emanated from labor quarters. There were no riots, no political upheaval, no episodes of civil disobedience; even the threatened strike failed to materialize.

Organized labor did not like the *Lochner* decision, but in its eyes, defeat in the courts was nothing out of the ordinary. This was one of the reasons why Samuel Gompers and other "pure and simple" labor leaders were cool to the idea of achieving labor's goals through legislation. They preferred collective bargaining and believed that if an organization was strong enough, it would be able to enforce the ten-hour workday without a ten-hour law. For them, therefore, developments in the baking industry over the next several years actually must have been somewhat gratifying. Even though a major strike of bakery workers never took place, a New York factory investigating commission was able to report in 1912 that where union conditions prevailed, the hours of work in the state's bakeries were limited to ten hours per day and sixty hours per week. Unorganized bakers, however, continued to work longer hours.

The *Evening Journal's* pronouncement that *Lochner* represented a sad day for labor legislation was misleading not only because organized labor was getting some of what it wanted, in the way it wanted but also because the Bakeshop Act was not "labor legislation" in the fullest sense of the phrase. Certainly it benefited an element of the labor population, but the major statewide and national labor organizations had not initiated the idea, nor had they lobbied for its enactment. If they supported it at all, they really had little choice. From the ranks of organized labor, only the Journeymen Bakers' and Confectioners' International Union of America had actively worked to pass the law. Its imposing name notwithstanding, that organization had a small and localized base of support, little money, and few resources. Its only strength was an energetic, articulate, and ambitious leader—Henry Weismann.

The political environment into which the proposal for bakeshop reform was cast in 1895 was not conducive to its adoption. New York's legislature was controlled by a machine that was philosophically opposed to the social and economic reform that it represented. It was even more a machine driven by practical politics, and there was no obvious practical reason to heed the call for bakeshop reform. The bakers' union, on the other hand, had little political power to give or to withhold. How could it have successfully pushed its favored bill through the process?

The answer is that it did not. Or, more precisely, it was not the bakers' union that was primarily responsible for enactment of the legislation. The bakers were involved, to be sure, but the idea of the Bakeshop Act grew out of the tenement-house movement. Journalist Edward Marshall's interest in improving the conditions of cellar bakeries created the opportunity. His link to influential mainstream reformers and the suitability of bakeshop reform to their agenda ultimately explains its successful enactment.

Mainstream reformers, whose influence had been essential to enactment of the Bakeshop Act in 1895, would not be assuaged by the quiet victories of union bakers following the *Lochner* decision. Tenement reformers, settlement-house workers, members of the National Civic Federation, people who participated in a wide variety of social reform organizations and who were to make up a large part of the Progressive movement, could not depend on strikes and collective bargaining to achieve their goals. They were more firmly attached to legislation as the means of ameliorating the oppressive social conditions that they thought existed. And it was for reformers that *Lochner v. New York* was to have the most lasting significance.

One reform periodical, *Outlook*, was quick to express concern. It maintained that with this decision, the Supreme Court usurped the legislative function to such an extent that it did not give the legislative branch of government the benefit of a doubt. Editors of *Outlook* feared that the ruling would tend to increase the power of radical labor leaders. They predicted that "those people of conservative tendencies who welcome this decision as a blow to Socialism and as a weakening of the power of labor unions will be disappointed." But this early comment by reformers did not see anything apocalyptic about the decision. The editors thought that with the judges equally divided, the decision would be applicable only to a particular method of regulating work in a particular occupation. The question of how far legislatures may interfere with individual contracts, they said, was still open for public and popular discussion.

The very nature of Supreme Court rulings gives them some impact beyond the immediate dispute between the parties involved, but the initial public reaction to the *Lochner* decision did not indicate that the case would have a special status in constitutional history. Its lasting significance was based upon something more subtle, and because it could not have been caused by the direct outcome of the decision, it must have arisen out of the ideas that it represented. Specific policy is not what ultimately made this case important. It reached a special status because of the Court's treatment of general principles.

Much of the reaction to *Lochner* reflected the argument made by Justice Harlan's dissent. Disagreement between Harlan and the majority existed within a framework of constitutional interpretation that they both accepted. Harlan was actually asserting that *Lochner* misapplied the majority's own theory. It had chosen to ignore facts weighing in favor of the statute's validity, and it had been too quick to violate the legislative prerogative.

Others in the legal profession continued this line of criticism. Two months after the case was decided, Professor Ernst Freund maintained that the tendency of courts to anoint themselves as censors of the legislative power had led to a growing uncertainty as to the limits of this power in the control of economic and social interests. The next month Sir Frederick Pollock, a British legal scholar and friend of Justice Holmes, questioned the logic of the Court's deciding the validity of this law when it knew little about the conditions affecting bakeries in New York.

Lay critics joined those within the legal profession in denouncing the decision for being technical and unrealistic. Speaking before the Quill Club in New York on the day after the decision was rendered, Samuel Gompers speculated that "if the majority of the court who signed the opinion had visited modern bakeries in this state, and had seen the conditions that prevail, even under the ten hour law, they would have believed that it was within the police powers of this state to regulate the hours."

"More than anything else," Roscoe Pound later wrote, "ignorance of the actual situations of fact for which legislation was provided and supposed lack of legal warrant for knowing them, have been responsible for the judicial overthrowing of so much social legislation." That ignorance, according to Pound, or at least the view that the judiciary was ignorant in that way, was caused in part by "mechanical jurisprudence." By this he meant a tendency to focus on the technicalities of law and the traditional legal distinction between law and fact. Ten years after the case was decided, Felix Frankfurter continued this line of attack in an article entitled "Hours of Labor and Realism in Constitutional Law." The court decided these issues on a priori theories, he observed, because scientific data were not available or at least not made available for their use.

These critics made a valid and important point. The judges who decided Joseph Lochner's case had not visited the cellar bakeries of New York City. Nor did the attorney general emphasize the working conditions in the baking industry in his defense of the statute. There is little question that judges at various levels voted on the basis of preconceived notions of what the job of baking entailed. Judge O'Brien, of the New York Court of Appeals, made this explicit by equating it with the life of "the good housewives of this state." Justice McKenna, one of the two justices whose change of mind had swung a majority of the Supreme Court to vote against the regulation, may have had a romanticized image of a baker's life as well. His father had been a successful baker in the small frontier town of Benicia, California.

This notion that the Court had ignored overwhelming facts about the perils of baking remains very much a part of the legacy of *Lochner*. Nevertheless, charges that the decision was the product of an unrealistic view of the conditions that gave rise to the law were exaggerated. The Court had before it Judge Vann's concurring opinion in the New York Court of Appeals, which provided enough sociological and scientific data to justify a conclusion that the state had a reasonable motive for passing the ten-hour ceiling. If these judges could not see the realities of life in the New York urban bakeshop, it was not so much because they were blinded by mechanical jurisprudence as because they had deliberately closed their eyes.

A chief concern of many critics within the legal profession was that decisions such as *Lochner* would ultimately erode respect for the courts and the law. By pointing to the problem of mechanical jurisprudence, they were able to provide the judicial system with an excuse while simultaneously attacking the result and proposing modification. Thus these critics proposed to introduce flexibility into the legal process and bring the court up to date.

The glaring subjectivity of the *Lochner* decision had much to do with eventually placing it in the limelight. The Supreme Court had so brazenly substituted its will for the will of the legislature that even people who were normally unlikely to publicly criticize the Court disagreed with the outcome and the way it was reached. Most critics realized that this aspect of the case would have been avoided if the Court had followed the reasoning of Harlan's dissent.

If this had been the only criticism of the majority opinion, *Lochner* would have represented nothing more than an isolated mistake; it would have been an aberration. But this was not the only criticism. Roscoe Pound saw something more in the Court's disregard of the facts. In articles written in 1907 and 1909, Pound observed a persistence of eighteenth-century natural-law theories in American legal thought long after they had been abandoned in other fields, as well as a sturdy resistance of common law individualism to the "collectivist tendencies of modern thought." He believed that these characteristics of legal thinking were responsible for decisions like *Lochner* and for a consequent loss of respect for the law.

Although the Court's apparent unrealistic view of the life of an industrial worker and the element of subjectivity made the *Lochner* case an inviting target, reformers made it clear from the start that they were more interested in the deeper theme developed by Pound. The Court had created a sphere in the field of social and economic reform in which neither the nation nor the state had effective control, they argued. Not only had the Court usurped a power properly abiding in the people, but it had strained the Constitution to the utmost "in order to sustain a do nothing philosophy which has everywhere completely broken down when applied to the actual conditions of modern life."

That philosophy had monopolized American economic and political thinking in the 1860s, 1870s, and 1880s. It was predominant in the years when the idea of a shorter workday first began to circulate. It was also the reigning theory of economics when Thomas Cooley and Justice Stephen Field began their efforts to fuse it into constitutional law. By the time the Bakeshop Act came into being in 1895, however, trends in economic thinking, and arguably the mood of the country, had begun to shift away from laissez faire–social Darwinism. It had been a decade since the New School of Economics, an organization of economists who rejected laissez faire, made its debut. Yet 1895 was also a year in which judicial resistance to economic and social legislation was very conspicuous, a year in which the Supreme Court invalidated the income tax and severely weakened the federal antitrust and interstate commerce acts. The degree to which the evolution of political and economic thinking was diverging from that of judge-made law was striking, and it became even more so following the reading of *Lochner v. New York* in 1905.

Some of this evolution in American thinking is reflected in the career of Theodore Roosevelt. As a state legislator in 1883, he sponsored a law that prohibited the manufacture of cigars in New York tenement houses. He did this despite a self-professed attachment to laissez-faire beliefs. On that occasion he acted not on the basis of a general theory but because of conditions that he had personally observed. By 1910 any attachment that Roosevelt had to laissez faire was severed. His political program, the New Nationalism, focused on a strong executive, more active regulation, and social welfare programs. Consequently his attack on the judiciary was directed at another level of unreality—the unreality of laissez faire in general and the laissez-faire interpretation of the Constitution in particular.

Roosevelt was not an unchallenged spokesman for reform. But in this respect he reflected the position of virtually all critics of the laissez-faire theory from the fields of politics, economics, philosophy, sociology, and law. These people had charged that survival of the fittest and laissez faire were not appropriate models upon which to organize the modern industrial community. With respect to liberty of contract, they pointed out that there was little or no equality of bargaining power between employer and employee. There were few contracts in any real sense of the word. The freedom that resulted from government inaction was but a shadow of liberty.

Mainstream reformers believed that the states had a duty to promote the general welfare and common good. In Roosevelt's words, they had a responsibility to shape social forces so as to benefit the material and moral well-being of the farmer and the wage earner, just as they should do in the case of business interests. Reformers believed that democracy offered the promise of fairness as well as liberty. To them laissez faire and the theory of the negative state were relics of the past that had taken up residence in the courts. There ensconced, these doctrines continued to frustrate the popular will and the development of a just society.

To Roscoe Pound the problem created by this link between eighteenth-century natural-law theory and legal thinking was more than one of results; it represented an error in method as well. Because of it, legal reasoning had become internal, seeking to enforce a fixed standard of justice that was completely divorced from the standard recognized by the rest of society. The result was an archaic and ineffective conception of the role of judges as being "passive oracles" who divined rules from an already existing body of legal principles. Pound claimed that this method persisted in law at a time when other fields had begun to shift to the natural and physical sciences. "Legal monks who pass their lives in an atmosphere of pure law, from which every worldly and human element is excluded," he charged, "cannot shape practical principles to be applied to a restless world of flesh and blood."

The Court's attachment to laissez-faire–social Darwinian theory and its disregard for the "scientific method" alarmed a generation of reformers. It would make *Lochner* a symbol through the Progressive Era and into the New Deal. In emphasizing these points, Roscoe Pound had vividly captured the significance of the case in the perspective of his time. But modern reformers have not been greatly concerned about the Court's adopting a laissez-faire philosophy, and they have become very adept in placing sociological and scientific fact before the judicial branch. Why then does modern reform remain haunted by the 1905 decision?

Roscoe Pound alluded to the answer in his essay on liberty of contract. "The sociological movement in jurisprudence," he explained, "was in part a movement for the adjustment of legal doctrines to human conditions they are to govern *and away from first principles.*" Admitting that this trend had scarcely shown itself in the United States, Pound noted that "perhaps the dissenting opinion of Mr. Justice Holmes in *Lochner v. New York*, is the best exposition of it we have."

Professor Ernst Freund echoed Holmes's theme when he speculated that even among those who think that such legislation is unwise or premature, there will be many who do not believe that it is opposed to the fundamental principles of the Constitution. Seven years later Theodore Roosevelt voiced the same concern. "I am not primarily concerned with . . . whether the extreme apostles of the laissez faire system . . . are right," he declared, "but I insist, as a matter of fundamental and primary concern, that we, the people, have the constitutional as well as moral right to try these experiments if we soberly determine to try them."

With the *Lochner* decision, the Supreme Court did more than reject an economic and social policy. It tabled consideration of the lines of moral reasoning advanced by reformers. By adopting the doctrine of liberty of contract and the narrow definition of the police power, it said that as a matter of fundamental law, promotion of public health, safety, and morals was the only legitimate motive for economic and social reform. Reformers not only had lost an important battle, they also had suffered a serious blow to the arsenal of arguments that they relied upon to convince the American people and their elected representatives of the righteousness of their cause. For many reform proposals the question became not whether problems would be wisely addressed, but whether they could be answered at all or whether they were taboo.

At the same time, the Supreme Court had seriously impaired the American decision-making process. Undeniably it had insulated certain issues from the impact of raw political power. This would have been beneficial and an essential element of the American system of government if those issues had been unequivocally addressed by the Constitution. But the experience of the *Lochner* case shows the opposite side of the coin. As the Court moved away from the letter of the Constitution, insulation of issues ceased to be beneficial. Instead the Court merely created a condition in which thorough debate on important public issues became practically futile.

Although the New York legislature did specifically consider the ten-hour ceiling, the Bakeshop Act's march through the legislative process does not prove that the theory of the shorter-hours movement was fully considered in that body either. Its enactment was very much a matter of politics. But mainstream reformers who supported the bill could not count upon raw political power, something of which they had little, to pass the law. Instead they relied upon public opinion, and it was in the competition for the ear of the public that the issues were more fully debated. There the theory of laissez faire–social Darwinism was only one of many moral theories and policy rationales that had come into play. A major impact of the *Lochner* case was that to the extent of the Court's influence on public opinion and the machinations of legislative bodies, laissez faire–social Darwinism would not need to depend entirely upon the strength of its reasoning in its competition with other theories. Instead it would be propped up by the exaggerated status that had been created for it by the Court.

Lochner v. New York left a legacy that few other cases can match. Some of the myths that grew around it have proved to be inaccurate. The absence of high-power attorneys weighs against the possibility that the case was part of a conspiracy perpetrated by the organized bar to infuse laissez faire into the Constitution. Given that the Court was not entirely isolated from the facts that instigated the ten-hour workday for bakers, mechanical jurisprudence does not entirely explain the decision. Finally, *Lochner* did not represent a struggle between labor and concentrated wealth, as has commonly been supposed. It involved a statute that was supported by prominent mainstream reformers and opposed by the owners of very small businesses. It is no myth, however, that the case and the Court were the bane of contemporary reformers—first of Progressives and then of the early New Dealers.

CHAPTER II

The *Lochner* Era

Outside the legal community, disdain for the *Lochner* decision did not fully materialize until 1910, when former president Theodore Roosevelt began a two-year barrage against the judiciary. Roosevelt's attack in a speech before the Colorado legislature on August 29, 1910, specifically used *Lochner* as an example of how the courts had frustrated the popular will. As he began an unsuccessful run to regain the presidency in 1912, Roosevelt developed the attack into a plan that provided for popular recall of state court decisions that invalidated legislation. Under this plan, judicial decisions holding state laws unconstitutional could be placed before the electorate and overruled by popular vote. Although state courts were the object of Roosevelt's plan, his scorn was equally directed at the United States Supreme Court. The nation's high court, he complained, had joined in throwing "well-nigh or altogether insurmountable obstacles in the path of needed social reforms."

One year later Charles Warren began a crusade to demonstrate that the Supreme Court was not the laissez-faire ogre reformers like the former president were making it out to be. In a somewhat crude empirical study, Warren found that in the years 1887 to 1911 the United States Supreme Court rendered over five hundred sixty decisions based on the due process and equal protection clauses of the Fourteenth Amendment. Of these, he claimed, only three cases involving "social justice legislation" resulted in the state statute being held unconstitutional.

Warren's study may have been flawed in several ways, but the point that more state statutes were upheld than overruled by the Supreme Court is irrefutable. More recent studies have added a degree of sophistication to this argument. John E. Semonche, for example, provides a term-by-term account of the years between 1890 and 1920. He concludes that although the Court claimed broad powers to oversee state legislation, it was not as conservative as depicted because it was hesitant to exercise that power. In a more specific study of cases concerning wages, working hours, employer liability, and worker's compensation, Melvin Urofsky concludes that the laissez-faire Court is a myth. Cases like *Lochner* and *Adair v. United States* (involving a statute prohibiting antiunion yellow dog contracts), he says, were exceptions to the general trend. Far from being an enemy of reform, the Supreme Court was as progressive as most reformers could desire. Other observers similarly argue that when the cases are counted, the judiciary did not prove to be hostile to regulatory legislation, antilabor, nor wholeheartedly in favor of big business, as it has traditionally been portrayed.

Important as these studies may be, they fail to explain why the judiciary, and the Supreme Court in particular, was the target of reformers' barbs from the late nineteenth century through the 1940s. One explanation is that the studies tend to focus on a period ending before 1920. Most concede that after that time the Supreme Court turned down a new, conservative path. But this does not go to the heart of the matter. Changes in the makeup of the Court between 1905 and 1937 affected the ebbs and flows—the fine-tuning—of Court decisions, but they did not drastically change the Court's direction.

By focusing on results, these empirical studies teach much about the impact of judicial decision making and the limits of the Court's power. Going beyond the great cases to examine the details of lesser-known case law is valuable in other respects as well. But determining the Court's direction involves more than a count of the decisions. By emphasizing results over reasoning, these studies tend to have misinterpreted that direction. Admittedly Roosevelt was wrong. The Court had not imposed an insurmountable obstacle to reform. The barrier through which reform legislation had to pass was something more like Ali Baba's cave. Beyond its entrance lay the police power. Many statutes were allowed to pass, but those that did not possess the right words were denied admission. And these words were "morals, health, safety, peace, and good order."

It is important to reemphasize that the idea of the police power as part of a schema of limitations on state authority did not exist before the Civil War. It had traditionally meant simply the power to govern. The notion of substantive due process and the doctrine of liberty of contract were also relatively new ideas. None of these concepts will be found in the words of the Constitution, and during the laissez-faire era they were not applied in anything like the traditional manner. John E. Semonche may be correct in observing that the Court used its newly developed powers sparingly, but his revelation loses much of its impact once it is understood that to many people, any application of this new power represented an unprecedented and unwarranted extension of judicial authority over state legislation. Semonche would have had a difficult time convincing reformers of the day of the Court's liberality. Those who had fought battles in the state legislatures for their view of fairness and justice, only to be foiled by what they viewed as an unjustified application of judicial power, were unlikely to be assuaged. These three doctrines were tightly linked. Substantive due process provided the judiciary with a vehicle for overseeing state legislation. Liberty of contract gave the Court an ideal, or value, to apply. It stood as a fixed standard but obviously could not be absolute. The police power was the variable and therefore the key to understanding the decisions of that era.

Attempts to define the limits of the police power reflected two differing views of the government's role. It did not reflect a battle over economic policy alone, and it was not solely a matter of protection of property versus government interference. It involved notions of liberty and fairness as well. Economics blended with moral philosophy to divide the contestants into two fuzzy but discernible sides. One emphasized business interests, individualism, the negative state, and status quo. The other leaned toward labor interests, collectivism, positive state action, and reform. The former, translated into "legalese" as Stephen Field's narrow definition of the police power, gained much ground in the late nineteenth century. But it took *Lochner v. New York* to firmly establish its dominance as Supreme Court precedent.

Even though some of the many state statutes upheld by the Supreme Court in the thirty years following *Lochner* surely were victories for reform, a close reading of case law during the period demonstrates that the Court never deviated from its ruling. Not only did it retain a veto over state legislation, but it retained it in such a way as to give reformers just cause for concern. That a state used its weight to assure fair dealings between parties of unequal bargaining strength would not save a statute from being charged with violating liberty of contract. That a statute attempted to ameliorate oppressive living conditions that grew out of industrialization would not justify interference with the right of property. State legislation challenged on the basis of the Fourteenth Amendment was approved only if it was deemed to promote the morals, peace and good order, or health and safety of the public.

———

The idea of public morals being subject to the police power remained much the same during the first third of the twentieth century as it had been in Stephen Field's day. State prohibition statutes, for example, continued to win court approval. One difference was that in the years following *Lochner*, cigarettes joined alcoholic beverages as the subject of Prohibition, and a somewhat prescient Minnesota law provided detailed regulation regarding the prescription and sale of habit-forming drugs.

Gambling and the supervision of sexual morality also continued to be subject to governmental action. Limitations on the sale of lottery tickets were approved in several instances. Regulation of pool halls—businesses that the Court observed to have a "tendency to lead towards that which is admittedly immoral and pernicious"—was also upheld. With respect to sexual morality the Court showed that it could be receptive to change by ruling that motion pictures could be censored.

The public-morals component of the police power continued to mean puritan morality and nothing more. It did not envision laws designed to promote fairness or good citizenship, nor did it envision laws that would in any way reorder the relationship between the advantaged and the disadvantaged in the newly industrialized society. One minor exception occurred in the 1920s, when post–World War I rent controls were approved as emergency measures. Even then, rent controls—like prohibitions against usury and fraud—tended to link traditional conceptions of morality with well-accepted notions of peace and good order. Statutes licensing trades and professions fell into this category as well. A law requiring applicants for a Tennessee real estate license to prove honesty, truthfulness, and competency, for example, was upheld even after the Court had passed into the more conservative period after 1920.

This combined motive had its limitations, however. Less conventional attempts to control avarice, gouging, and advantage taking were often successfully attacked as violations of due process and liberty of contract. State laws regulating private employment agencies provide a prime example. The United States Bureau of Labor found that abuses were rampant in this business. In a 1912 study it reported that employment agencies commonly collected fees far out of proportion to services rendered, failed to make any effort to find work for the applicants, misrepresented terms of employment, and induced workers to pay bribes. Nevertheless, when a Washington State law prohibiting fees charged to job seekers came before the Supreme Court in 1917, it was overruled.

———

Another component of the police power is made up of cases dealing with "peace and good order." This phrase has been borrowed from Stephen Field's opinion in *Munn v. Illinois* because it is most descriptive of an ill-defined concept. In truth, however, different justices used a variety of phrases, including general welfare, public welfare, and general prosperity, to convey this idea. In legal parlance it was sometimes said to be guided by the Latin maxim *"sic utere tuo ut alienum non laedas,"* which when translated—"so use your property as not to injure the property of others"—proves to be nothing other than a version of Herbert Spencer's first principle. Whatever the phrase, however, the laissez-faire–social Darwinian understanding of peace and good order prevailed. This component of the police power simply recognized the law's age-old role of protecting property and providing rules to smooth the flow of commercial intercourse or to settle disputes between owners of property.

It is not surprising that statutes fitting into this category were approved by the Supreme Court. What is startling is that so many found their way to the nation's highest tribunal at all. Rather than demonstrating that the Court was receptive to change, as some modern historians claim, the very presence of so many cases involving remarkably conventional functions of government shows how deeply the idea of laissez faire–social Darwinism had been imbedded in the constitutional psyche.

The establishment of standard weights and measures, for example, has forever been a basic governmental function. It would take a pretty extreme individualist to charge that government had stepped beyond the bounds of propriety in setting a standard weight for a loaf of bread. Yet this is precisely what was claimed in the 1913 case *Schmindinger v. Chicago*. And when the state of Missouri passed a seemingly inoffensive rule requiring that "every sale of grainseed, hay, or coal shall be made on the basis of actual weight," it was also attacked as a violation of due process. Both of these measures were later upheld, but the wonder is that their constitutionality was ever seriously disputed.

The weights-and-measures aspect of other cases was sometimes less glaring. Ohio and Arkansas, among other states, passed laws requiring that miners' wages be computed on the basis of the weight of coal before screening. Workers believed this to be a fairer computation because it reduced the possibility that they would be cheated by an enlarged or worn mesh screen. Employers charged that these laws violated liberty of contract, and they took their case to the Supreme Court. Upholding the statutes, the Court noted that "laws tending to prevent fraud and require honest weights and measures in the transaction of business have frequently been sustained by the courts, although in compelling certain modes of dealing they interfere with freedom of contract." No doubt such statutes bore the mark of reform, but they were upheld as conventional applications of the police power. The regulations may have resulted in better wages, but no extension of state power resulted from the Court's approval. Justices Brewer and Peckham dissented nevertheless, and although similar laws were upheld in the first ten years following *Lochner*, the Court never abdicated its right to review them. The door was left open for the more conservative Court of the 1920s, when in *Burns Baking Co. v. Bryan* (1924) even the innocuous regulation of the weight of a loaf of bread was no longer safe.

A second category of peace and good order allowed the state to promulgate regulations designed to encourage efficient operation of commercial intercourse and to promote the general prosperity. Broad though this power may seem, it shares with other aspects of peace and good order an attachment to the maxim *sic utere tuo ut alienum non laedas*. Thus quarantines of livestock, regulations on sheep grazing, and penalties for allowing fast-growing Johnson grass and Russian thistle to proliferate along railroad lines were upheld. Plans that would encourage and protect investment, such as a Connecticut law designed to protect creditors by requiring struggling retailers to give notice before selling their entire stock in bulk, passed as well.

State governments had much latitude, but with respect to peace and good order, the Court once again retained the power to veto statutes that a majority of its members thought had gone too far. What is more, it did so on a significant number of occasions between 1905 and 1920. A Kentucky statute requiring that railroads deliver livestock to connecting carriers, an order that railroads install switches to certain grain elevators, a Texas law requiring that train conductors have two years' experience, a requirement that streetcars be heated, and a regulation regarding the use of unoccupied upper berths in sleeping cars were all invalidated as unreasonable extensions of the police power.

Although some regulations in this category were upheld and others overruled, the progress of one case in particular made it quite evident that the majority of justices had no intention of expanding the idea of peace and good order, or any other component of the police power, beyond what it had settled on in *Lochner. Noble State Bank v. Haskell* involved an Oklahoma law that created, and required banks to contribute to, a depositors' guarantee fund. Arguing against the constitutionality of the statute, opponents claimed that it amounted to an unlawful taking of private property. The Court disagreed. Justice Holmes was tabbed to write the majority opinion and did so in sweeping language reminiscent of his dissent in *Lochner*. "It may be said in a general way that the police power extends to all public needs," he wrote. "It may be put forth in aid of what is sanctioned by usage or held by the prevailing majority or strong and preponderant majority to be greatly and immediately necessary to the public welfare."

Here, as an explicit precedent in a majority opinion, was all reformers could hope for. This definition of the police power made room for their ideals of fairness, and it was broad enough to allow the state to use its weight in attempts to assure fairness in the economic and social order. Victory was fleeting, however. Later that

　　　　{ *Lochner v. New York* }

same year Noble State Bank petitioned for a rehearing. Although the petition was denied, Holmes was persuaded to recant on his expansive description of the police power. The analysis of this power in the original opinion, he now agreed, "whether correct or not, was intended to indicate an interpretation of what has taken place in the past, not to give a new or wider scope to that power." In other words, the former statement was nothing more than his personal view. As far as the majority was concerned, nothing had changed.

By the 1920s state efforts to bolster the general prosperity or to provide order in the marketplace were met with an even more restrictive view of the police power. A Pennsylvania statute aimed at the problem of subsidence of the surface caused by mining coal was invalidated, and other attempts to regulate the trucking, banking, railroad, and insurance industries also fell under the constitutional axe. One case, *Truax v. Corrigan,* illustrated that the Court was not completely averse to allowing the state to throw its weight into the bargaining between employees and employers. But from the view of organized labor and reformers, the *Truax* decision, which invalidated a statute forbidding the use of injunctions against picketing, threw that weight squarely on the wrong side.

Statutes meant to provide orderly methods of settling disputes constituted another conventional subcategory of peace and good order. This group included rules for litigation as well as rules that encouraged settlement without litigation. In 1904, for example, a state mechanics' lien law was upheld against the claim that it offended liberty of contract. Even more imaginative efforts, such as a Nebraska law that provided a fixed measure of damages to livestock owners whose shipments had been delayed by railroads, were successfully defended. But decisions went the opposite way as well. Between 1905 and 1920 a Kansas statute providing five hundred dollars as liquidated damages for overcharging on shipments of oil was invalidated; Arkansas's rule that a railroad pay double damages for failure to settle claims for killing livestock and a similar South Dakota provision were overruled; and a Missouri statute forbidding insurance companies from forfeiting policies after three years of premiums had been paid was held unconstitutional. The pattern continued. A decade later state efforts to curb abuses by such means as creating presumptions against railroads or limiting insurance companies' ability to reduce their exposure to liability were also ruled unconstitutional.

Even during its period of relative liberality, the Court continued to exercise the power to review laws concerning peace and good order. It did not hesitate to invalidate statutes when a majority believed the state had stepped beyond the vague laissez-faire–social Darwinian boundaries that marked the limits of the police power. The justices' position only intensified after the Court made a more conservative turn in the early 1920s.

———

The Supreme Court's record dealing with early employer liability and workers' compensation laws is sometimes said to make a strong case for the proposition that the Court was receptive to change. In the last few decades of the nineteenth century and the first part of the twentieth, almost every state passed legislation that altered the existing rules governing industrial accidents. Some were challenged on Fourteenth Amendment grounds as violations of liberty of contract or deprivations of property without due process. Although state courts invalidated some plans, most that made it to the Supreme Court were upheld.

Because nineteenth-century common law rules were thought to greatly favor employers, the Court's acquiescence to these modifications is offered as proof that the Court was receptive to change. This conclusion is surely accurate in some respects. Many of the Court's rulings must have pleased reformers. But the legal theory upon which these decisions rested did not demonstrate that the Court had become farsighted or liberal, nor that it had abandoned its laissez-faire–social Darwinian leanings. What it does show is that statutory changes in the law governing industrial accidents fell squarely within the narrow definition of the police power that the Court itself had created.

Three nineteenth-century common law doctrines handicapped workers who hoped to recover damages from their employers after having been injured on the job. Contributory negligence absolved the employer of all liability if it could be proven that the injury was to any extent caused by the worker's own negligence. Assumption of the risk relieved the employer of much liability under the theory that the worker knew of, and agreed to take responsibility for, dangers inherent in a job. Finally, the fellow servant rule buffered the employer from liability whenever an injury had been caused in part by a coworker. The last of these rules received the greatest attention both in case law and in commentary and accurately represents the experience with all three.

Common law rules are not a product of legislation. The term refers to a body of law that develops in the courts over a period of time. The fellow servant doctrine was no exception. Applied repeatedly in individual cases, it became an established part of the legal system. This particular rule had not been long established, however. Early in the nineteenth century, responsibility for damages caused by the negligence of a worker during the course of employment was guided by an entirely different doctrine—*respondeat superior* (let the master answer)—which assigned liability to the employer. The fellow servant rule originated in the English courts in 1837 and was developed in American courts during the middle of the century. This new doctrine reversed the presumption of *respondeat superior*, but only when injury was suffered by another person working for the same employer.

The logic advanced in favor of the fellow servant rule definitely bore the mark of economic individualism. All things being equal, workers would choose the least dangerous jobs available, it was argued. Therefore employers would have to pay higher wages for more dangerous work. Compensation for the risk of injury had already been determined by the forces of the marketplace.

Policy reasons were also forwarded in favor of the fellow servant rule. By reducing the amount of litigation, the rule was thought to encourage growth in the business community. Workers' exposure to pecuniary loss under the rule was said to reduce accident rates by making them more careful on the job. The change was said to be justified because *respondeat superior* resulted in injustice by assigning liability without negligence. In other words, employers had been responsible for injuries that were not directly their fault.

The logic against the fellow servant rule and other common law rules also has a familiar ring. Reliance on market forces to assure that workers would receive adequate compensation for injury or the risk of injury was said to be unrealistic. Workers had no bargaining power; they accepted jobs that were available. Nor did workers have control of the workplace or their fellow employees. Besides, with the development of huge corporations, virtually everyone was an employee. There was no identifiable master to be held responsible for safety on the job. This resulted in undue hardship on the worker, who for all practical purposes was without recourse. Thus family and society would be saddled with the burden of those injured on the job.

Those favoring changes in the common law defenses turned the policy rationale for insulating employers from liability on its head. They predicted that when exposed to damages for the acts of their employees, employers would take greater care to hire and train careful people. A response was available to the jurisprudential rationale as well. It pointed to the numerous examples of assigning liability without negligence that already existed in common law, not the least of which was *respondeat superior.*

Strong sentiment against the rule produced two distinct results. First, exceptions to the common law defenses developed gradually through judicial interpretation. A rule called the vice-principle exception, for example, placed liability back on the employer's shoulders when injury resulted from the negligence of an employee who stood in a supervisory position. Another exception made employers somewhat responsible for maintaining a safe workplace, by declaring that certain duties could not be delegated.

Popular sentiment also pressured state legislatures to enact statutes abolishing the common law defenses entirely for some lines of work. Laws passed by Kansas and Missouri made their way to the United States Supreme Court, where they were upheld in 1888. Employers' claims that the changes in common law doctrine constituted the taking of property without due process and a denial of equal protection were curtly dismissed in a pair of short opinions written by Justice Field. The father of laissez-faire constitutionalism expressed no doubt that promulgation of laws that reversed the standing legal doctrine governing industrial accidents was well within the power granted to state legislatures.

Although one cannot be certain, Field might have sought a different result if he had been sitting in a state legislature. The status of the fellow servant rule, contributory negligence, and assumption of the risk surely represented a battle between competing economic views, and their abolition marked defeat for the side with which Field is usually associated. Normal inclinations led employers to hope the judiciary would reverse this trend, but the Constitution was the wrong theater in which to continue the fight. The reason is elementary: these common law doctrines were not based upon any constitutional right, nor upon any natural right for that matter. They did not take property nor limit its use. They amounted to nothing more than judicially created rules of law that created presumptions and assigned the burden of proof to be applied in a dispute.

The reason underlying Field's complete confidence that modification of these rules was well within the police power was stated even more emphatically by Justice William Moody in a later opinion. Moody began by explaining the status of the common law rules, which he described as judicial opinions guided by the judges' views of what justice and sound policy demanded. He noted that even when these opinions crystallized into well-settled doctrines of law, they were binding only on succeeding judges. They did not control legislatures, nor did they acquire constitutional sanctity. "They are simply rules of law, unprotected by the Constitution from change, and like all other such rules must yield to the superior authority of a statute."

Abolition of the common law defenses was never seriously challenged on due process grounds. The *Employers' Liability Cases* of 1908 involved an act of Congress that negated the fellow servant rule and contributory negligence in cases involving injuries to the employees of common carriers. This act was overruled because it could be interpreted to apply to injuries occurring while a worker was not directly engaged in interstate commerce. The majority held that it was therefore beyond the power vested in Congress by the commerce clause.

Even lawyers for the railroads conceded that statutes abolishing the fellow servant rule were within the police power. In their opinion that was the very reason Congress had no right to legislate on this subject. "The Employers' Liability Act is not a regulation of commerce at all," they argued. "It relates simply to one of the ordinary relations of life—and the legal rules affecting such relations are within the control of the states."

Two years later Congress passed a second Employers' Liability Act, which cured the problems relating to interstate commerce. This time the Supreme Court upheld the act. Justice Willis Van Derventer's majority opinion responded to the claim that the new law was unwarranted interference with liberty of contract: "A person has no property, no vested interest in any rule of common law. . . . Rights of property which have been created by common law cannot be taken away without due process; but the law itself, as a rule of conduct, may be changed at will by the legislature."

Although the constitutionality of abolishing the common law defenses was beyond question, the problem of how to compensate victims of industrial accidents was not yet solved. Changes in the common law rules shifted the legal burdens, but the system remained a system of risk. The chance of financial and legal recovery was increased significantly for injured workers, but it remained just that—a chance. A favorable award sometimes depended upon how skillful the lawyers were and how appalling the injury might appear to a jury. Zero recovery was always a possibility. Even when a worker did win, payment was likely to be seriously delayed, and a large amount of the victory went to attorney's fees. Employers were equally dissatisfied. The common law system was unpredictable, especially when the defenses supplied by the fellow servant rule, contributory negligence, and assumption of the risk were abolished. Juries often seemed disposed to be sympathetic to injured workers, and awards large enough to put a company out of business were always a possibility.

Seeking a more predictable and fair method of dealing with injuries on the job, both reformers and business interests eventually looked to the workers' compensation plan pioneered in Germany in the 1880s. Under most workmen's compensation plans, as they were then called, injured workers were paid a fixed sum of money based on the type of injury and lost earnings. This award was made without regard to fault. Payment came from an insurance fund that was generally created by employer contributions and run by the state.

In this system there would be no lawyers' fees, no delay, no zero recovery, no devastating losses; and the cost to employers was predictable. The problem was that workmen's compensation involved government to a greater extent than did simply changing rules of law. It smacked of regulation. As Louis Brandeis observed, abolition of the common law rules did not mark a departure from the individualistic basis of right and liability, but workmen's compensation did—thus the opposition to it.

New York passed the first workmen's compensation law in 1910. During the next two years, at least ten more states followed its lead. The original New York plan lasted only about one year, however. In 1911 it was invalidated by the state's highest court. Judge Werner, who wrote the New York opinion, conceded that the state had authority to abolish the employer defenses. But substituting a system of workmen's compensation was to him another matter entirely. "One of the inalienable rights of every citizen is to hold and enjoy property until it is taken from him by due process of law," he reasoned. "When our constitutions were adopted it was the law of the land that no man who was without fault or negligence could be held liable for injuries sustained by another." Judge Werner concluded that having done just this, the workmen's compensation law violated both federal and state due process guarantees.

This was an ingenious line of reasoning. Though based upon procedural arguments, it sought to create a new fundamental right against which judges could test the substance of state legislation. The only hitch was that Stephen Field had long before shown that liability without fault did exist under common law. Judge Werner's assessment of legal precedent was simply wrong. His attempt to create a new constitutional right—freedom from liability without fault—never gained much favor and was rejected by the United States Supreme Court in the first workmen's compensation case it considered.

New York Central R. R. v. White involved New York's second effort to create a workmen's compensation plan. The state's new plan, along with similar laws passed by Iowa and Washington, was tested in the Supreme Court in 1917. Each was upheld in separate opinions written by Justice Mahlon Pitney. Pitney implied that completely replacing the old common law system of assigning liability for injuries on the job was not a significantly different exercise than changing the rules within that system. "The common law bases the employer's liability for injuries to the employee on the ground of negligence, but negligence is merely the disregard of some duty imposed by law," he wrote. The nature and extent of that duty could be modified by legislation, whether it changed the test for negligence or created liability based upon a statutory duty irrespective of negligence.

Viewed in this way, workmen's compensation statutes fell cleanly into the laissez-faire–social Darwinian idea of peace and good order. The state had merely exchanged one set of rules governing the settlement of disputes for another. But an additional characteristic of the New York plan probably helped soothe those who were uncomfortable with the idea. Unlike its predecessor, the new statute did not require that employers join the state insurance plan. They retained the option of insuring through a private company or self-insuring and depositing a bond as security.

An even more obvious reason why the New York statute represented a reasonable exercise of the police power was that it dealt with the health and safety of those to which it applied. Although all workmen's compensation laws theoretically fit into this category of the police power, the New York statute possessed a characteristic that satisfied even the most reticent of the justices: it applied only to specifically designated hazardous trades.

These two characteristics—the voluntary nature of the plan and its application to hazardous trades—were important in the cases that followed. In *Hawkins v. Bleakly* a unanimous Court upheld the Iowa statute that, although not limited to hazardous trades, was optional. In *Mountain Timber Co. v. Washington* the justices had more difficulty agreeing on the validity of a statute that was compulsory but applied only to hazardous jobs. They upheld the Washington plan by a 5 to 4 margin.

These 1917 workmen's compensation cases did not expand the definition of the police power beyond that upon which the Court had settled in *Lochner.* If it changed at all, it was narrowed. As late as 1938, legislatures continued to pay homage to the idea that compensation laws would be valid only if applied to specified dangerous trades, while commentators continued to say that workmen's compensation would be improved by judicial approval of universal and compulsory plans.

Arizona later enacted a statute that was somewhat different. Like the New York and Iowa plans, it allowed employers the option of self-insuring, but it did not substitute the workmen's compensation plan for the old common law rules. Instead a worker injured in certain dangerous jobs was given a choice of receiving a fixed amount under the workmen's compensation plan or seeking recovery for damages in the courts. The worker's own negligence would bar recovery in the courts, but the common law defenses of assumption of the risk and the fellow servant rule were abolished.

Part of the rationale for workmen's compensation, the part that made it attractive to employers, was its predictability and avoidance of high awards by the jury. The Arizona law plainly defeated that goal. Employers made this point when the Arizona plan came before the Supreme Court. Because the worker was free to reject the fixed compensation provided by the workmen's compensation law, they complained, employers were deprived of their common law defenses and given nothing in return. Justice Pitney, who appeared to have become the Court's specialist on workmen's compensation cases, once again wrote the opinion of the majority. In it he rejected the idea that validity of compensation schemes depended upon such a quid pro quo. A narrow 5 to 4 decision allowed the Arizona law to stand.

Dissenting opinions, marked by scattered traces of laissez-faire-social Darwinian rationale, were written by Justices McKenna and McReynolds. To McReynolds the various grounds offered in support of the Arizona law amounted to nothing more than an assertion that the legislature had the power to protect society against the consequences of accidental injuries. Taking a liberty-of-contract stance, he objected that this view presupposed that the resulting loss may be imposed wholly without fault upon employers "who have afforded others welcomed opportunity to earn an honest living under unobjectionable conditions." Placing the burden on employers, added McKenna, ultimately deprived them of a fair return on their investment. He recognized that the motives of Arizona's legislature might have been worthy, but he objected to the plan because "individual rights cannot be made to yield to philanthropy. . . . The difference between the position of employer and employee, simply considering that latter as economically weaker, is not justification for the violation of the rights of the former." The nature of the Arizona plan and the tone of the dissents invite a conclusion that reformer ideology had carried the day. Quite to the contrary, however, what is known about the Court's deliberations on the matter vividly illustrates that the majority declined to join any march in the direction of expanding the state's role in leveling social or economic inequities.

Holmes, not Pitney, was originally slated to write the opinion. But the sweeping language of his draft, reminiscent of that which he had used in *Nobel State Bank v. Haskell,* risked breaking up the fragile majority in favor of upholding the statute. Holmes thought that it was reasonable that the public should pay the entire cost of the products it wanted. "By throwing the loss upon the employer in the first instance we throw it upon the public in the long run and that is just. If a legislature should reason this way and act accordingly it seems to me that it is within constitutional bounds." Sensing a rejection of the Holmes draft, Brandeis prepared a dissent. This dissent, which took pains to trace the tradition of laws creating liability without fault, represented a tactful argument in favor of the statute. Its publication was made unnecessary, however, when Holmes agreed to offer his draft as a concurring opinion and Pitney was assigned the task of writing for the majority.

In the end it was the cautious approach that held the majority. Pitney pointed out that the Arizona statute did not present any unique issue. Like the New York, Iowa, and Washington workmen's compensation laws, it was merely a reversal of the common law burden; it differed only in degree. Furthermore it applied only to hazardous trades. Regardless of whether this law amounted to bad policy, Pitney concluded that it was not arbitrary, unreasonable, nor unconstitutional.

If workmen's compensation amounted to a victory for reformers, the Supreme Court's acquiescence assured that they would savor that victory. But judicial recognition of the constitutionality of new laws governing industrial accidents did not require liberalization. The Court had not altered its thinking with regard to the limits of the police power.

———

Nothing more clearly reveals the boundary that the Supreme Court drew around the state police power than the events of 1908. In that year the Court ruled on the famous "case of the overworked laundress"—*Muller v. Oregon.* The *Muller* case is remembered primarily for Lewis Brandeis's novel brief, which emphasized sociological and scientific data in support of a state shorter-hours law. It is significant because the Supreme Court upheld the statute. Coming a mere three years after *Lochner*, it represented a major courtroom victory for reform.

The *Muller* decision might be explained, however, by the fact that liberty of contract applied only to persons who were *sui juris*—that is, persons who possessed legal capacity to manage their own affairs. Justice Peckham based much of his logic for the *Lochner* decision on the contention that bakers were equal in intelligence and capacity to men in other trades and were thus able to assert their rights and care for themselves without the protecting arm of the state. Women and children, on the other hand, were not equally capable in the turn-of-the-century conservative mind. Nor were they deemed *sui juris* in early twentieth-century law. Proponents of laissez faire objected to paternalistic regulations that interfered with adult men in the conduct of their own affairs, but even so radical an advocate as William Graham Sumner believed that the duty of government was to "protect the property of men and the honor of women."

Muller v. Oregon involved a statute that controlled the working hours of women. Ultimately the Court's approval turned as much upon special concern for the health of women as upon their inferior legal status. But the case did not repudiate *Lochner*. Brandeis's sociological data simply demonstrated how the Oregon law fit into the laissez-faire framework. Justice Brewer, who wrote the *Muller* opinion, had not modified his opposition to the "paternalistic theory of government." The Court had not given up its veto over state legislation, and it had not abandoned the laissez-faire doctrine.

As if to drive home the point, in the same term that *Muller* was decided, the Court overruled a federal statute that outlawed antiunion yellow dog contracts in interstate railroads. That case, *Adair v. United States*, showed how deeply rooted the doctrine of liberty of contract had become. The author of the Court's decision was John Harlan. The justice who had so staunchly emphasized that the Court should begin with the presumption that legislative determinations were valid had apparently reached his limit. Harlan may have been inclined to defer to the legislative judgment, but he also accepted the narrow definition of the police power. He could see nothing in the yellow dog contract that affected the health, safety, or morals of the community. A pattern for the next decade of decisions had been established. In 1915, for example, the Court invalidated a state yellow dog contract prohibition. But in cases involving women's hours and other statutes that were unmistakably matters of health and safety, it tended to defer to the judgment of state legislatures.

Reformers watching the Supreme Court in 1917 could find substantial cause for optimism. In addition to the series of cases upholding workmen's compensation laws, the Court ruled in *Wilson v. New* that when emergency conditions existed the federal government could set an eight-hour day for workers on interstate railroads. The most significant decision of the term, however, was *Bunting v. Oregon*, which tested the constitutionality of a ten-hour statute. The Oregon statute before the Court in this case differed from the one upheld in *Muller* in two respects: it applied to all persons employed in a mill, factory, or manufacturing establishment—men as well as women and children; and it allowed for up to three hours of overtime work but required that a rate of time and a half of the regular wage be paid for that period.

Directing the defense of the statute, Felix Frankfurter bolstered his legal arguments with sociological and statistical data in much the same manner as Brandeis had done in *Muller*. Once again the method proved successful. In an opinion written by Justice McKenna, the Court upheld the ten-hour law and gave optimistic reformers cause to believe that *Lochner* had been implicitly overruled.

A decision rendered just one year later, however, should have given them pause. In *Hammer v. Dagenhart* the Court invalidated a federal child labor law. This decision was based upon a narrow reading of the commerce clause and therefore had little to do with the precedent of *Lochner*, but it signified that the negative state and the ideal of laissez faire-social Darwinism had not yet been abandoned by the United States Supreme Court. Indeed, several years later Felix Frankfurter would once again be called upon to defend a law regulating the conditions of labor, and this time he would lose. In *Adkins v. Children's Hospital* the court overruled a federal statute that created a minimum wage for women and children working in the District of Columbia.

To some extent vacillation in the outcome of cases from *Lochner* to *Bunting* and then to *Adkins* may have been the result of chance and of changes in the personnel of the Court. Surely these factors came into play, but once the philosophical underpinnings of the

Lochner decision are brought into light, a common thread tying these cases together becomes obvious; it becomes equally clear that *Lochner* had not been overruled.

Given the facts of *Bunting*, one might reasonably have concluded that the Court had at least reverted to the rule applied in *Holden v. Hardy* and *Atkin v. Kansas* and championed by Harlan's dissent in *Lochner*. The very breadth of the new Oregon ten-hour statute that the Court was sanctioning hinted that it was now willing to defer to legislative judgment as to what constituted a reasonable application of the police power. But had the burden of proof once again shifted? Was the Court thereafter going to begin its deliberations with the assumption that state regulatory laws were valid? The language of the *Bunting* opinion was not quite that definite. "There is a contention that the law . . . is not necessary or useful for the preservation of the health of employees," wrote Justice McKenna. "The record contains no facts to support the contention." This was all he said on the matter. It could be that the Court was applying the Harlan test. But it could also be that using the device of the "Brandeis brief," Frankfurter had simply been able to satisfy a majority of the Court that the statute involved in this case was reasonable for the protection of public health and safety.

Regardless of its potential implications, and regardless of what Justice McKenna may have intended, nothing about *Bunting* committed the Court to the principle that an act of a state legislature should be presumed valid. Six years later, writing for the majority in *Adkins*, Justice Sutherland made this quite explicit. "Freedom of contract," he declared, "is . . . the general rule and restraint the exception; and the exercise of legislative authority to abridge it can be justified only by the existence of exceptional circumstances." Given the large number of regulatory statutes affirmed by the Court in the early twentieth century, it is tempting to make light of Sutherland's declaration. To do so is to miss an important point. Sutherland was not counting cases. He was reaffirming the Court's commitment to a principle — one that emphasized the limit of state authority to intercede in social and economic relationships.

The constitutional expression of that principle was captured in the narrow definition of the police power adopted in *Lochner*. Here was the element that tied the seemingly disparate decisions of the first third of the century together. Though the Court showed outward signs of somewhat stretching the police power, in every case in which liberty of contract came into play, state law was matched against a test of whether it protected public health, safety, morals, or peace and good order. Thus in the majority's opinion, mining and smelting were dangerous trades and warranted an exception to the general rule against regulation; baking was not. Yellow dog contracts had nothing to do with health and safety, and women, being viewed as inferior beings, were the proper subject of work-hour limitations to protect their health.

Bunting seemed to represent an expansion of legislative discretion, and maybe it did. By the time it came before the Court, however, the ten-hour day was common enough to be considered customary. Minimum wage was destined to become the subject of the next battle, and despite Oregon's time-and-a-half provision, the Court went to great lengths in emphasizing that the law was nothing more than a regulation of working hours. Requiring time and a half for overtime, it said, was merely a means of enforcement. Like the cases before it, *Bunting* turned on the majority's acceptance of the state law as a legitimate health regulation. Throughout the 1920s the Court would be consistent in overruling state efforts to establish a minimum wage or even to require arbitration to resolve wage and hour disputes.

Some say that *Bunting* illustrates that the justices rarely interposed the Constitution as a barrier that could not be overcome by the imagination and dedication of those serving the public interest. The point is well taken, but it exudes the wrong emphasis. What is important is that reformers of the era still had to pass through the police-power hoop fabricated by the Supreme Court. And they seemed to be well aware of the restriction by which their efforts were bound. The District of Columbia minimum wage law challenged in *Adkins v. Children's Hospital* contained language that could have served little purpose other than to help it along the legal gauntlet. Section 23 declared that "the purposes of the act are to protect women and minors of the District from conditions detrimental to their health and morals, resulting from wages which are inadequate to maintain a decent standard of living."

Frankfurter's defense of the statute also emphasized its connection to public health. He argued that Congress had found widespread existence of a deficit between the essential needs of a decent life and the actual earnings of large numbers of women. In its judgment, "these conditions impaired the health of this generation of women and thereby threatened the coming generation through undernourishment, demoralizing shelter, and insufficient medical care." Convincing though Frankfurter's argument might have been, for the majority of the Court the connection between earnings and health was too far removed to justify a minimum wage law.

In a manner pertaining more directly to reform measures generally, Frankfurter also argued that a minimum wage did not "shock the sense of fairness the Fourteenth Amendment was intended to satisfy." The technique of appealing to fairness was not without precedent—it was a consideration in many due process cases. When a state was deemed to have authority to regulate rates charged by a business affected with public interest, for example, the due process clause required that those rates assure a fair rate of return. But Frankfurter had another conception of fairness in mind, one that would allow the power of the state to be used to achieve social goals. The line of cases upholding limitations placed upon freedom of contract, he argued, rested upon a realization that the mass of women workers cannot secure terms of employment needful from the point of public welfare without the weight of legislation being thrown into the scales. This was, of course, the opinion of an advocate. The notion of due process that had developed over half a century of cases imposed fairness as an additional *limit* on state regulation. It did not necessarily follow that fairness was an acceptable *reason* for state action.

The argument that a contract could be neither free nor fairly entered into when one party held all the cards may have been persuasive as a moral or political argument, but the justices who made constitutional law were not impressed. Laissez faire–social Darwinism continued to dominate the high court's picture of reality. Justice Pitney expressed the majority position in unmistakable terms. "No doubt, whenever the right of private property exists, there must and will be inequalities of fortune," he wrote. But to him this did not justify striking down the rights of liberty and property "by declaring in effect that public good requires removal of those inequalities that are but a normal and inevitable result of their exercise."

The majority in *Adkins*, it turned out, was to hold true to this version of fairness. Justice Sutherland observed that "the basis of the minimum wage law was not the value of the services rendered to the employer, but the extraneous circumstances that the employee needs to get a prescribed sum of money to insure her subsistence, health, and morals." This, he concluded, completely ignored "the moral requirement implicit in every contract of employment, viz., that the amount to be paid and the service to be rendered shall bear to each other some relation of just equivalence." In other words, the employer was entitled to a fair return on the contract, a sum that could only be determined by the free play of the market.

More than a decade after the District of Columbia's minimum wage law was invalidated, the attorney general of New York attempted to turn this language on its head by arguing that a minimum wage law was the only means by which women could secure a fair rate of return for their services. In 1936 most of the justices were not yet ready to be swayed. But one year later, in *West Coast Hotel v. Parrish*, the Court suddenly reversed its position. Upholding a Washington State minimum wage law, it expressly overruled both the fresh opinion regarding the New York law and *Adkins v. Children's Hospital.*

The majority opinion, written by Justice Charles Evans Hughes, was an unabashed expression of a reformer's view of fairness. "The exploitation of a class of workers who are in an unequal position with respect to bargaining power and are thus relatively defenseless against the denial of a living wage is not only detrimental to their health and well being, but casts a direct burden for their support upon the community." "What the workers lose in wages, the taxpayers are called upon to pay," he continued, "and the community is not bound to provide what is in effect a subsidy for unconscionable employers. The bare cost of living must be met." Hughes also drew a new boundary for the police power, declaring that "peace and good order may be promoted through regulations designed to insure wholesome conditions from work and freedom from oppression." Coming thirty-two years after the ruling in *Lochner, West Coast Hotel v. Parrish* signified that the preeminence of liberty of contract and laissez faire–social Darwinism was at an end.

CHAPTER 12

Epilogue

With his appointment of eight justices to the Supreme Court between 1937 and 1943, Franklin D. Roosevelt undoubtedly hoped to assure that the *Lochner* Era was safely buried. The president was partially successful. His appointees were more sympathetic than their predecessors to his economic platforms. They fully rejected the doctrine of liberty of contract and with it the pervasive judicial oversight of plans for economic reform.

Roosevelt's long-running dissatisfaction with judicial overstepping also played a role in his choice of nominees. The new justices were chosen partially because they were opposed in principle to judicial activism. Most had been critical of the Supreme Court for having broadly interpreted the Constitution to achieve particular social goals and for being too quick to interfere with the legislative prerogative by overruling statutory law. If FDR also hoped that his judicial appointments would result in a permanent reduction of the Supreme Court's power, he fell short of his goal. The new Court's renunciation of judicial activism was not as emphatic nor as enduring as its acceptance of the New Deal.

West Coast Hotel v. Parrish had hardly been set into print when the Court hinted as much in *United States v. Caroline Products*. Decided in 1938, *Caroline Products* applied a test for reviewing state legislation that was similar to Harlan's dissent in the *Lochner* case. Writing for the majority, Justice Stone declared that regulatory legislation affecting ordinary commercial transactions was not to be pronounced unconstitutional unless it was of such character as to preclude the assumption that the legislature had acted upon some rational basis. But, said Stone in his now famous footnote four, there may be circumstances in which the presumption is reversed. From this afterthought arose a double standard that surely would have sent a shiver down the spines of Justices Field, Peckham, and Brewer. A presumption favoring the validity of state legislation existed when economic regulation was at issue, but a stricter standard would be applied when other "preferred freedoms" or "personal liberties" were at stake.

No one in the twentieth century had ever argued that the Court should be without authority to review the substance of state legislation under the due process clause. Even Holmes accepted some degree of substantive review and understood that the judges' personal beliefs would be part of the decision-making process. What Holmes had argued in *Lochner* was that the Court's use of that power should be restrained and that it certainly should not be used to create new fundamental rights. In the first two decades following *West Coast Hotel v. Parrish* this attitude dominated the Court. During that time the Court was divided on how to apply the due process clause. Just what these "preferred freedoms" were that would subject a state statute to "strict scrutiny" was the subject of some heated debate. Justices Cardozo and Frankfurter favored a "fundamental fairness" test that rejected only those statutes that threatened the "very essence of a scheme of ordered liberty." Justice Black believed that the due process clause of the Fourteenth Amendment "incorporated" the first eight amendments of the Bill of Rights, thus making them applicable to the states. But the precedent of *Lochner*—to the extent that it represents a tendency to find new fundamental rights under the umbrella of due process—was rejected by all. The bête noire of reform now served only as a stark reminder of past wrongs.

This new attitude was conspicuous when in 1963 the Court heard an appeal from a U.S. district court that had ruled that a Kansas law restricting the business of debt adjustment violated the due process clause. Noting that the doctrine that prevailed in *Lochner* and similar cases had long since been discarded, Justice Black virtually scolded the district court for its backwardness. "We emphatically refuse to go back to the time when courts used the Due Process Clause to strike down state laws, regulatory of business and industrial conditions, because they may be unwise, improvident or out of harmony with a particular school of thought," he wrote. "Whether the legislature takes for its textbook Adam Smith, Herbert Spencer, Lord Keynes, or some other is no concern of ours." But would the Court refuse to so act when considering legislation regulating social or political rather than economic conditions? Would it be inclined to look to sociology, psychology, or other disciplines outside the field of economics to find justification for striking down such laws?

The answer became evident just two years later when, in *Griswold v. Connecticut*, the Court overruled an antiquated prohibition on dispensing contraceptives or providing advice or counseling with respect to their use. In a short opinion for the majority, Justice William O. Douglas found residing in the First, Fourth, and Fifth Amendments a "right of privacy." This right, he said, was further secured by the Ninth Amendment, which guaranteed that rights not enumerated in the Bill of Rights were retained by the people. Douglas was not clear about how this right was made applicable to the states, but he carefully and expressly avoided turning to the due process clause for support. Justice Goldberg was almost as elusive in his concurring opinion. "While the Ninth Amendment—and indeed the entire Bill of Rights—originally concerned restrictions upon *federal* power," he wrote, "the subsequently enacted Fourteenth Amendment prohibits the states as well from abridging fundamental personal liberties."

To Justice Black all of this was a charade. He thought the majority had created a new fundamental right and had applied it to the states via the due process clause of the Fourteenth Amendment, and he chided them for being afraid to cite the precedent upon which they really relied—*Lochner* and its genre. Black's dissent carried his own agenda. He was advancing his theory that the Fourteenth Amendment incorporated the Bill of Rights and did nothing more. But he also made a graphic point. The reasons offered in support of the Court's protecting an individual's right of privacy bore an eerie resemblance to the justifications of laissez-faire constitutionalism.

At the turn of the century, proponents of liberty of contract had argued that the intended role of the Court was to protect individuals from the tyranny of the majority. For people such as William D. Guthrie, Christopher Tiedemann, and Thomas Cooley, substantive due process and liberty of contract represented not only reasonable but necessary interpretations of the Constitution. In their eyes the theory of law that was finalized in *Lochner* was supported by the spirit and purpose of that document. Their position emphasized that judicial interpretation should be flexible enough to allow the Constitution to keep up with changing times. The argument was shored up with appeals to "the rule of reason." George W. Wickersham, who had been attorney general during the Taft administration, explained that the rule of reason was a method of protecting the liberty provided for in our fundamental law of the Constitution and harmonizing it with the imperative needs of civilized society. Implicit in this idea was the belief that the Court should be an activist in its guardianship of fundamental rights. "When the judiciary no longer feels at liberty to construe provisions of fundamental law in the light of reason," Wickersham continued, "constitutional government, in the sense which it has been understood for a century and a half, will be at an end."

Critics of the laissez-faire Court, emphasizing the extraconstitutional nature of the legal theories supporting *Lochner* and similar cases, called for a return to a strict interpretation of the Constitution. They argued that the Court should make its decisions on the basis of the "four corners" of the Constitution, or the intent of the framers. The bakeshop case provided them with a graphic illustration of the contrademocratic nature of the Court's power of judicial review. In no other Supreme Court decision was the will of the majority of the people more glaringly frustrated by what seemed to be nothing other than judicial fiat. Cries that the country was being ruled by an "imperial judiciary" or "judicial veto" and calls for judicial restraint were often punctuated with references to *Lochner v. New York.*

The essentials of this debate remain intact today. What has changed, however, is that from the 1960s to the late 1980s the Court's activism moved in a new direction, causing interests that had assumed one stance in the laissez-faire era to ease over to the opposite leg. Contemporary views of the Court's role have been influenced by the experience of the recent past, during which the Court used an aggressive and imaginative interpretation of the Constitution to achieve liberal goals. The right of privacy that was established in *Griswold* served as the basis for the Court's decision to overrule a state law prohibiting abortion in *Roe v. Wade.* This, along with decisions regarding racial discrimination, voting rights, religious freedom, and criminal justice, has resulted in a tendency to equate judicial activism with political liberalism. Yet the legacy of *Lochner* continues. Those among today's reformers who still see the judiciary as the ultimate guardian of personal liberty are faced with the unenviable choice of accepting its legitimacy or trying to distinguish their version of judicial lawmaking from that embodied in *Lochner v. New York.*

If what proponents of a double standard are seeking is something in the "spirit" of the Constitution that justifies treating economic and noneconomic liberties differently, the history of ideas of which *Lochner* is a part demonstrates that the distinction is not there. In light of *Griswold* it is not difficult to accept the idea that a broad right of privacy exists in the spirit of the Constitution. But just as Douglas might have been correct in observing that personal privacy is a right that emanates from the spirit of the Constitution, so others might have been just as correct in their claim that the right to choose an occupation or the right to the unrestrained use and benefit of personal property resides in that incorporeal domain.

———

Conflicts involving the spirit of the Constitution nevertheless occasionally need to be resolved. Thus some modern scholars justify judicial activism by pointing out that the Court provides the best forum in which to do this. Their view may well be correct when a governing principle is explicit or readily discoverable in existing fundamental law. However, the story of *Lochner v. New York* illustrates that this optimistic vision of the judicial process loses much of its luster when competing principles are involved or when the Court sets out to achieve some lofty goal without pitons securely anchored into the Constitution.

Idiosyncrasies of legal reasoning and the legal method may, on the contrary, render the judiciary ill suited for this function. In 1909 Roscoe Pound complained that a reasoning peculiar to judicial decision making—mechanical jurisprudence—was responsible for excesses in applying the doctrine of liberty of contract. Years later, Justice Robert Jackson made a similar complaint, noting that unrealistic judicial decisions are brought about in part by the convenient "fictions," or assumptions of fact, employed in the legal method. Others have pointed out that *stare decisis*, the revered rule of judicial interpretation that requires that decisions be based upon rulings in past cases, can produce convoluted reasoning when the Court attempts to justify a change of opinion. The precedent of *Lochner*, for example, explains much of the circuitous reasoning in *Griswold*. Besides, history certainly has not shown the judiciary to have a monopoly on dealing adequately with matters of principle. Clifton McCleskey convincingly made this point by asking, "Which of the Civil War Justices excelled Lincoln in voicing the hopes and goals of the Republic?"

The belief that the Court is the most likely branch of government to deal properly with matters of moral principle and to move the nation in the direction of truth stands in stark contrast to Oliver Wendell Holmes's dissent in *Lochner v. New York*. Michael J. Perry, one of the proponents of this theory, attempts to explain the difference by emphasizing that he is speaking about human rights and that his view of the Court is influenced by the experience of the past twenty-five years. Stating that the decisions in *Dred Scott* and *Lochner* are merely examples of mistakes made by a fallible judiciary, he warns that we should resist specious historical generalizations about the performance of the Supreme Court. Those who dare to risk being charged with antiquarianism, however, will find the historical excursion anything but empty. If we hope to determine whether there is something inherent in the operation of the Supreme Court that ensures increased dialogue—something that makes it the best forum for discovering of the truth or for choosing among competing moral principles—then we would do well to remove the blinders fastened by our own experience. The historical events that spawned the *Lochner* case, along with the theories and politics that converged in that decision and the complaints that resulted from it, suggest that the view of the Court as "the forum of principle" is romanticized.

―――――

Other modern scholars maintain that the judges of the *Lochner* era did not merely attach laissez-faire-social Darwinian ideals to the Constitution. According to this school of thought it is more accurate to depict the decisions of the era as the heirs to an age-old American tradition of liberty: one that is reflected in ideals of pre-Civil War social and political doctrines such as Jacksonian Democracy and the free-labor movement. The judicial decisions of the *Lochner* era may have been conservative, backward, unsettling, or even wrong to Progressive and New Deal reformers. But they were not unsettling or wrong because judges molded their own set of beliefs into constitutional doctrine. They were unsettling because these age-old visions of liberty and traditions of individualism clashed with the realities of modern industrialized America. Thus, according to Howard Gillman, rather than being an example of the Court's overstepping its role in democracy, the *Lochner* era was a crisis in American constitutionalism. The crisis was settled when, beginning in 1937, the Roosevelt court rejected the *Lochner* era's version of economic individualism.

This theory has the advantage of providing those modern liberals who still attach their hopes to the judiciary with a means to reject the *Lochner* era's economic interpretation of the Constitution while, at the same time, espousing judicial activism. One problem with the theory, however, is that it overstates the connection between pre–Civil War ideals of liberty and the ideals of laissez faire–social Darwinism. There is no doubt that we find in the cases and opinions commonly associated with laissez faire a genuine commitment to liberty. The theory of laissez faire is after all a theory founded on a certain kind of economic liberty. But the story of *Lochner v. New York* demonstrates that the more poignant question is not one of liberty or no liberty, but rather a question of what kind of liberty and for whom.

The version of liberty found in laissez-faire constitutionalism emphasizes a desire to be free from government interference. A similar antigovernment theme permeated Jacksonian Democracy. But focusing on the antigovernment theme oversimplifies the Jacksonian ideal. The reason for this is that while government neutrality was the central theme of laissez-faire constitutionalism, it was only one of a hierarchy of Jacksonian ideals.

Of these ideals, individual liberty sat at the top. But to Jacksonians liberty did not mean merely freedom from government intervention. It carried with it a vision of self-sufficiency—a vision that also feared oppression at the hands of an economic elite.

This fear of oppression at the hands of an economic elite led to the second in the hierarchy of Jacksonian values: opposition to special privilege. The Jacksonians expressed their disdain for special privilege by attacking what they called "moneyed interests." This does not mean that Jacksonians opposed property rights. They were not even opposed to wealth if it was accumulated by hard work and prudence. What they were opposed to was artificial wealth—that is, wealth acquired from influence or power. In the Jacksonian picture of society, the source of this artificial wealth was usually government. Jacksonians saw government as an instrument doling out special privileges to an influential elite. Jacksonians feared special privilege because it tended to concentrate power and thus warp the natural working of a democratic society. In the Jacksonian mind, special privilege created a vicious cycle that threatened the liberty of common individuals.

A desire for limited government was the third tenet of Jacksonian Democracy. But it is important to understand that the Jacksonians' distrust of government stemmed from their fear of special privilege.

The Jacksonian idea of limited government, while sounding similar, was thus quite different from the laissez-faire idea of limited government. Jacksonians did not fear government regulation. They didn't even think in terms of their liberty being threatened by government regulation. The Jacksonians' ultimate goal was to limit the threat that moneyed interests posed to their liberty. They saw government as the hand that fed these moneyed interests. And they wanted to limit government, as one observer put it, "in order to starve that monster in its cradle."

Laissez-faire constitutionalism did employ antigovernment themes with rhetoric similar to Jacksonian Democracy's. The two do share a concern for liberty in the broadest sense of the word. But the history of the *Lochner* case shows how laissez-faire constitutionalism turned the Jacksonian ideals on their head. Where the Jacksonians opposed economic privilege, the laissez-faire emphasis on protection of property and liberty of contract tended to protect economic privilege. Where Jacksonians wanted to purify the workings of democracy, laissez faire feared the workings of democracy. Where Jacksonians tended to be egalitarian, the outcome of laissez-faire constitutionalism tended to be elitist.

———

There is yet another group of legal scholars who, setting the tone for a modern property rights movement, call for a return to the reasoning of *Lochner*, to the doctrine of economic substantive due process, and to the Court's role in assuring limited government. Justice Peckham's decision in *Lochner* reflected ideals that the founders had in mind as they debated the Constitution, argues Bernard Siegan. The framers of the Fourteenth Amendment also intended to include economic liberties among those protected by the due process and equal protection clauses. To Siegan, as well as some other constitutional scholars, *Lochner* was correct not only as a matter of constitutional law but also as a matter of sound economics. After observing that Holmes's dissent contained some of the most lauded language in legal history and explaining that his position has been consistent with modern federal law, Siegan tells us that recent history has shown that the Holmes perspective has not favorably influenced the human condition. Instead, he says, the economic marketplace has been so overwhelmed by regulation that freedom of property and even Holmes's marketplace of ideas have been all but lost.

Taking the baton, Ellen Frankel Paul argues that the police power should be limited to instances of protecting the public health and safety, or at least the burden of proving economic regulations to be constitutional should be shifted back to the government. "Who if not the courts," she asks, "stand as the final bulwark against government's propensity to seek the public good at the expense of trenching upon property rights?"

A new conservative Supreme Court has responded. In several cases like *Nollan v. California Coastal Commission* (1987), *Lucas v. South Carolina Coastal Council* (1992), and *Dolan v. City of Tigard* (1994), the Court has recognized a theory that is to the modern day what liberty of contract was to the laissez-faire era. Where the laissez-faire-era theory of property rights turned to the Fourteenth Amendment and maintained that economic regulations violate an individual's liberty of contract, the new theory turns to the takings clause of the Fifth Amendment. Proponents of this new theory maintain that any economic regulation can constitute a taking of an individual's property and thus must comply with the Fifth Amendment's requirements that the government can take individual property only for a public use and that the owner must receive just compensation.

Although based on different provisions of the Constitution, in many significant ways the new theory and the old are the same. Both would make the right of free exchange, or something like it, a constitutional right. And both envision a system in which government's only legitimate function is to provide an atmosphere in which economic individualism can flourish. Richard Epstein, the most influential advocate of the new theory, makes the link clear when he describes the limits of government power. The sole function of the police power, Epstein explains, is to protect individual liberty and private property. Private rights may be modified only to serve external and internal peace. How does one determine which state laws are a legitimate exercise of this function? Epstein seems to have found his answer in Herbert Spencer's quill: "The police power as a ground for legitimate public intervention is, then, exactly as when a private party acts on its own behalf. The individual who demands protection against takings by others loses that protection when he himself takes or threatens to take property." In order to assure that the state does not exceed its authority, Epstein also proposes that courts return to the burden of proof required in *Lochner*. The state should be able to show that there is a rational relationship between any regulation and the legitimate ends it claims to achieve.

Many Americans today believe that the time for a rebirth of classical economics has come. Even from that vantage point, however, a full appreciation of the *Lochner* experience—the events and theories that made it important, the Harlan and Holmes dissents, and the controversy that it stirred—demonstrates why fusing neoclassical economics into the Constitution would not make good constitutional law. The story of *Lochner v. New York*, and of the theories, politics, and events in which it was embroiled, provides an enlightening contrast to the more recent history of the judiciary's impact on American politics. For that very reason it enriches our understanding and should help to extract political preferences from our opinions about the proper role of the Supreme Court.

Contrasting the Holmes and Harlan dissents should raise some troublesome questions for those who are convinced that the desire for judicial restraint is satisfied by confining the Court to a search for original intent. To those who admire the Court for its flexibility and its efforts to bring the Constitution up to date, the *Lochner* case should serve as a reminder of the consequence if those efforts fall short. By the time the Court had embraced laissez faire–social Darwinism, those theories were, in the eyes of its critics, at least half a century out of date. Furthermore, the Court's adoption of laissez faire–social Darwinism, theories that claimed to do nothing more than allow natural order to take its course, should make us wary of doctrines that claim to be value-neutral. The background of the *Lochner* case also demonstrates that rather than assuring that important social issues are fully and fairly debated, the misuse of judicial review can skew the tenor of those debates by abating the force of reasonable rationales and excluding crucial options from the realm of possible outcomes. Finally, modern reformers, who have gamboled through several decades of liberal judicial activism, certainly must now be wary of having left the door open for a revival of some variation on the earlier activism as the makeup of the Court changes—just as many conservatives must be pleased at the prospect that *Lochner* is not dead.

CHRONOLOGY

1867–1868	Illinois, Wisconsin, Missouri, Connecticut, New York, and Pennsylvania pass the first eight-hour laws. These laws simply declare eight hours to be a legal workday. The United States Congress passes a similar measure for federal employees.
1868	The Fourteenth Amendment to the United States Constitution is ratified. Thomas McIntyre Cooley publishes the first edition of his influential treatise, *Constitutional Limitations.*
1872	The *Slaughter-House Cases:* In its first effort to interpret the Fourteenth Amendment, the Supreme Court rejects the theory that the amendment prohibits the state of Louisiana from requiring New Orleans butchers to practice their trade in a central slaughterhouse. Justices Stephen Field and Joseph Bradley write forceful dissents that lay the foundation for the theories of substantive due process and liberty of contract.
1877	*Munn v. Illinois:* Upholding an Illinois law that established maximum fees for storage in grain elevators, the Supreme Court recognizes the power of states to regulate "businesses affected with public interest." In doing so, however, it tacitly adopted the theory of substantive due process.
1885	*In re Jacobs:* In the so-called cigar makers' case, New York's highest court overrules a state statute that prohibits manufacturing cigars in tenement house dwellings. It bases its decision on the theory of liberty of contract. Richard T. Ely, Henry Carter Adams, Edmund James, and other members of the "new school of political economics" form the American Economic Association.

May 3, 1886	The Haymarket Riot: labor unrest leads to the death of several police officers and the conviction and execution of several so-called anarchists.
1887	Thomas Collier Platt begins his reign as boss of New York State's Republican party. Platt remained in control until the turn of the century.
1888	Edward Bellamy's *Looking Backward* is published. This utopian socialist novel inspires the formation of hundreds of Nationalist Clubs.
1893	Henry Weismann arrives in New York to become editor of the *Bakers' Journal*. Within one year he becomes the virtual leader of the Journeymen Bakers' and Confectioners' International Union of America.
1893-1894	The Panic of 1893 sets off a deep economic depression. With 24.9 percent of the nation's workers unable to find employment, thousands join Coxey's Army to march on Washington, D.C.
1894	The Tenement House Committee of 1894, called the "Gilder Committee," begins its investigation of New York City's slums. The good government movement leads to the formation of the "Committee of Seventy" to investigate New York City's Democratic machine, "Tammany Hall." This, in turn, leads to a coalition between Republican boss Platt's statewide machine and urban reformers.
September 30, 1894	Edwin Marshall, Sunday editor of the *New York Press* and member of the Gilder Committee, publishes the first of his exposés of tenement cellar bakeries.
October-November 1894	Henry Weismann and a committee of journeyman bakers presents a petition calling for the New York legislature to address the problems of cellar bakeshops. The petition does not mention a ceiling on the hours of labor in bakeries.

{ *Lochner v. New York* }

1895	New York passes the Bakeshop Act, which, among other things, limits the hours of work in the bread-baking industry to not more than ten hours per day or sixty hours per week.
February 12, 1895	Assemblyman Arthur Audett introduces the Bakeshop Act in the New York State Assembly.
March 19, 1895	The Bakeshop Act passes the assembly by a unanimous vote of 120 to 0.
April 1, 1895	The Bakeshop act passes the state senate by a vote of 20 to 0.
April 1895	Fearing that the language of the act might restrict the hours that bakery owners could work in their own shops, Governor Levi P. Morton sends the Bakeshop Act to the legislature for reconsideration. With new language applying the shorter-hours provision to employees only, the bill again passes by a unanimous vote of 90 to 0 in the assembly and 29 to 0 in the senate.
May 2, 1895	Governor Levi P. Morton signs the Bakeshop Act.
June 1895	Riding his success in passing the Bakeshop Act, Henry Weismann is elected the international secretary of the Journeyman Bakers' Union, thus officially becoming the labor union's leader.
1896	*Holden v. Hardy:* The United States Supreme Court upholds a Utah law placing an eight-hour ceiling on the workday of miners and workers in smelters and refineries. The Court observed these jobs to be dangerous trades.
1897	*Allgeyer v. Louisiana:* This is the first case in which the United States Supreme Court explicitly recognizes the theory of liberty of contract.
Autumn 1897	Caught skimming money paid by advertisers to the *Bakers' Journal,* Henry Weismann is

forced to resign as head of the Journeyman Bakers' Union.

Between 1897 and 1901, Wiesmann opens several cellar bakeries of his own. He becomes active in the Retail Bakers' Association and joins with other boss bakers in attempts to weaken the Bakeshop Act of 1895.

1899   Statistics show that 78 percent of bread-baking shops employ four or fewer people. The earliest mechanical improvements for bread baking have been discovered, but still only 10 percent of the bread-baking industry is mechanized.

1900   The National Civic Federation is formed for the express purpose of improving relations between labor and capital by promoting moderate reform.

1901   Handling minor cases in the Brooklyn Police Court, Henry Weismann is accused of unauthorized practice of law. No record exists that Weismann was at that time, or any other time, admitted to the bar in New York State.

1902   On February 12, bakeshop owner Joseph Lochner is convicted of causing one of his employees to work more than 60 hours in a week in violation of the New York Bakeshop Act. Lochner is sentenced to pay fifty dollars or to spend fifty days in jail.

Lochner's trial attorney, William S. Mackie, files for appeal in the appellate division of the New York Supreme Court (the state's intermediate court of appeals).

The appellate division upholds Lochner's conviction by a vote of 3 to 2, thus recognizing the validity of the Bakeshop Act. Lochner appeals to the next level, the New York Court of Appeals.

1903   *Atkins v. Kansas:* The United States Supreme Court, by a vote of 6 to 3, upholds an eight-hour limit on the workday of government employees and the employees of government contractors.

1904	The New York Court of Appeals, the state's highest court, upholds Joseph Lochner's conviction by a vote of 4 to 3. Henry Weismann takes over Mr. Lochner's case. Weismann asks Lochner's former attorney to file a notice of appeal to the United States Supreme Court. Henry Weismann secures the help of attorney Frank Harvey Field in the appeal of Lochner's case to the Supreme Court. Weismann is listed on the records as "of counsel."
November 1904	Julius M. Mayer is elected attorney general of the State of New York. With only a few months until oral arguments, Mayer takes over the *Lochner* case from former attorney general John Cuneen.
February 23, 1905	Oral arguments are heard in *Lochner v. New York*.
April 17, 1905	The United States Supreme Court overturns Joseph Lochner's conviction by a 5 to 4 vote. Writing for the Court, Justice Rufus W. Peckham reasons that the Bakeshop Act interferes with the liberty of contract between employer and employee. Justices John Harlan and Oliver Wendell Holmes write forceful dissents.
1905-1937	The *Lochner* case begins a period of Supreme Court history often referred to as the "*Lochner* Era" or "laissez-faire constitutionalism."
1908	*Muller v. Oregon:* The Supreme Court upholds a state law limiting the working hours of women.
1917	*Bunting v. Oregon:* The Supreme Court upholds a statute that sets the workday at ten hours but provides for overtime pay at time and a half of the regular wage.
1918	*Hammer v. Dagenhart:* The Supreme Court

invalidates a federal law aimed at prohibiting child labor.

1923   *Adkins v. Children's Hospital:* The Supreme Court overrules a federal statute that created a minimum wage for woman and children working in the District of Columbia.

1937   *West Coast Hotel v. Parrish:* Marks the end of the *Lochner* Era. Upholding a Washington State minimum wage law, the Supreme Court rejects liberty-of-contract doctrine and expressly overrules *Adkins v. Children's Hospital.*

BIBLIOGRAPHICAL ESSAY

Note from the Series Editors: The following bibliographic essay contains all the primary and secondary sources the author consulted for this volume. We have asked all authors in the series to omit formal citations in order to make our volumes more readable, inexpensive, and appealing for students and general readers. In adopting this format, Landmark Law Cases and American Society follows the precedent of a number of highly regarded and widely consulted series.

This book is an updated and slightly revised version of Paul Kens, *Judicial Power and Reform Politics: The Anatomy of Lochner v. New York* (Lawrence: University Press of Kansas, 1990). The earlier version contains detailed scholarly citations and references to case law.

Howard Gillman, *The Constitution Besieged: The Rise and Demise of Lochner Era Police Powers Jurisprudence* (Durham, N.C.: Duke University Press, 1993) and Owen M. Fiss, *Troubled Beginnings of the Modern State, 1888-1910*, Oliver Wendell Holmes Devise History of the Supreme Court of the United States, vol. 8 (New York: Macmillan Publishing Company, 1993) are excellent recent works that provide an alternative view of the *Lochner* case and the *Lochner* Era.

Although there has not been much work done on the history of the baking industry, Hazel Kyrk and Joseph Stancliffe Davis, *The American Baking Industry, 1849-1923* (Stanford, Calif.: Stanford University Press, 1925), and William G. Panschar, *Baking in America*, 2 vols. (Evanston, Ill.: Northwestern University Press, 1956), provided useful accounts. Tuberculosis, by contrast, has been a popular topic of study. Older works I found useful are Rene Dubos and Jean Dubos, *The White Plague* (Boston: Little, Brown and Company, 1952), and Arthur J. Myers, *Captain of All These Men of Death* (St. Louis: Warren Green, 1977). A more recent study of the disease is provided in Katherine Ott, *Fevered Lives: Tuberculosis in American Culture Since 1870* (Cambridge, Mass.: Harvard University Press, 1997).

David Montgomery, *Beyond Equality: Labor and the Radical Republicans, 1862-1872* (New York: Alfred A. Knopf, 1967), provides a relatively modern study of the shorter-hours movement. Older studies are provided by Marion Cotter Cahill, *Shorter Hours: A Study of the Movement since the Civil War* (New York: Columbia University Press, 1932); Elizabeth Brandeis, "Labor Legislation," and Don D. Lescohier. "Working Conditions," in *History of Labor in the United States, 1896-1932*, 4 vols., ed. John R. Commons et al. (New York: Macmillan Company, 1935). George Gunton, "Feasibility of an Eight Hour Day," *American Federationists*, July 1894; George Gorham Groat, "The Eight Hour Movement and Prevailing Rate Movement in New York State," *Politica*

Science Quarterly, July 1906, pp. 414-33; Samuel Gompers, *The Workers and the Eight-Hour Workday, and the Shorter Workday: Its Philosophy* (Washington, D.C.: American Federation of Labor, n.d.); and Lemuel Danryid, *History and Philosophy of the Eight-Hour Movement* (Washington, D.C.: American Federation of Labor, 1899), provide even more contemporary discussions of the movement.

Among the studies I found most useful on Boss Platt and New York politics at the turn of the century are these: Thomas Collier Platt, *The Autobiography of Thomas Collier Platt*, ed. Louis J. Land (New York: B. W. Dodge and Company, 1910); Harold Gosnell, *Boss Platt and His New York Machine* (Chicago: University of Chicago Press); Richard L. McCommick, *From Realignment to Reform: Political Change in New York State, 1893-1910* (Ithaca, N.Y.: Cornell University Press, 1979); and David C. Hammack, *Power and Society: Greater New York at the Turn of the Century* (New York: Russell Sage Foundation, 1982). For treatment of the civic reformers, see Gerald Kurland, "The Amateur in Politics: The Citizens' Union and the Greater New York Mayoral Campaign of 1897," *New York Historical Society Quarterly* 53 (October 1969): 352-84; Kurland, *Seth Low* (New York: Twayne Publishers, 1971); Gerald W. McFarland, *Mugwamps, Morals and Politics, 1884-1920* (Amherst: University of Massachusetts Press, 1975); and Richard Skolnik, "Civic Group Progressivism in New York City," *New York History* 51 (1970): 411-39.

I made the connection between the Bakers' Union and New York City's civic reformers by reading issues of the *Bakers' Journal* from early 1894 to 1896 and Edward Marshall's articles in the *New York Press* in 1894 and 1895. General treatment of civic reform can be found in Roy Lubove, *The Progressives and the Slums: Tenement House Reform in New York City, 1890-1917* (Pittsburgh: University of Pittsburgh Press, 1962); Irwin Yellowitz, *Labor and the Progressive Movement in New York State, 1897-1916* (Ithaca, N.Y.: Cornell University Press, 1965); Howard Lawrence Hurwitz, *Theodore Roosevelt and Labor in New York State, 1880-1900* (New York: Columbia University Press, 1943); and Marguerite Green, *The National Civic Federation and the American Labor Movement, 1900-1925* (Washington, D.C.: Catholic University of America Press, 1956).

American economics of the late nineteenth century is reflected in Francis Wayland, *Elements of Political Economy* (Boston: Gould, Kendall, and Lincoln, 1845); Arthur Latham Perry, *Elements of Political Economy* (New York: Charles Scribner's Sons, 1873); Edward Atkinson, *The Industrial Progress of the Nation* (New York: Arno Press, 1973, rpt. of 1889 ed.); and Atkinson, *Labor and Capital, Allies Not Enemies* (New York: Harper and Brothers, 1877). For the most significant works espousing social Darwinism, see Herbert Spencer, *Social Statics*, abridged and revised, with *The Man versus the*

State (New York: D. Appleton and Company, 1897); William Graham Sumner, *What Social Classes Owe to Each Other* (Caldwell, Idaho: Claxton Printers, 1952, rpt. of 1883 ed.); and Sumner, *Folkways* (New York: Gin and Company, 1906); for an overview, see Richard Hofstadter, *Social Darwinism in American Thought*, revised ed. (New York: George Braziller, 1959).

Irving Howe, *Socialism and America* (New York: Harcourt Brace Jovanovich, 1895); Charles A. Madison, *Critics and Crusaders: A Century of American Protest* (New York: Henry Holt and Company, 1947); and Howard Quint, *The Forging of American Socialism* (Columbia: University of South Carolina Press, 1953), provide useful overviews of socialism in America. Morris Hillquit, *Socialism in Theory and Practice* (New York: Macmillan Company, 1912, rpt. of 1909 ed.); Daniel DeLeon, *Socialist Landmarks* (New York: New York Labor News Company, 1952); and Edward Bellamy, *Looking Backward* (New York: Penguin Books, 1984, rpt. of 1888 ed.), are examples of some of the turn-of-the-century socialist writings.

The political and economic theory of what I call mainstream reformers is found in Richard T. Ely, "The Past and Present of Political Economy," vol. 2 in *Johns Hopkins University Studies in Historical and Political Science*, ed. Herbert B. Adams, 80 vols. (Baltimore: John Murphy and Company, 1884); Washington Gladden, "Socialism and Unsocialism," *Forum*, April 1887; Edmond Kelly, *Evolution and Effort* (New York: Macmillan Company. 1895); and Felix Adler, *The World Crisis and Its Meaning* (New York: D. Appleton and Company, 1915).

Traditional legal historians (some scholars refer to them as Progressive historians) explain the *Lochner* Era as an effort to implant laissez-faire economic theory into the Constitution. Representative of these works are Benjamin R. Twiss, *Lawyers and the Constitution* (Princeton, N.J.: Princeton University Press, 1942); Howard J. Graham, *Everyman's Constitution* (Madison: State Historical Society of Wisconsin, 1968); Clyde E. Jacobs, *Law Writers and the Courts* (Berkeley and Los Angeles: University of California Press, 1954);. Carl Brent Swisher, *American Constitutional Development* (Boston: Houghton Mifflin Company, 1943); and Robert Green McCloskey, *American Conservatism in the Age of Enterprise, 1865-1910* (New York: Harper and Row, 1951). Bernard Schwartz, *A History of the Supreme Court* (New York: Oxford University Press, 1993), is one more recent work that demonstrates the traditional view is still alive. For the work of Thomas M. Cooley, I used Thomas M. Cooley, *Constitutional Limitations* (Boston: Little, Brown and Company, 1868). For a different view of Cooley, see Allen Jones, "Thomas M. Cooley and Laissez Faire Constitutionalism: A Reconsideration," *Journal of American History* 53 (1967): 751.

For examples of modern historians who maintain that the cases of the *Lochner* Era have roots in pre-Civil War traditions, see Charles W. McCurdy,

"Justice Field and the Jurisprudence of Government-Business Relations: Some Parameters of Laissez-Faire Constitutionalism, 1863-1897," *Journal of American History* 61 (1975): 970-1005; Charles W. McCurdy, "The Roots of 'Liberty of Contract Reconsidered: Major Premises in the Law of Employment, 1867-1937," *Yearbook of the Supreme Court Historical Society* (1984): 20-33; Michael Les Benedict, "Laissez-Faire and Liberty: A Re-Evaluation of the Meaning and Origins of Laissez-Faire Constitutionalism," 3 *Law and History Review* 293 (fall 1985); Howard Gillman, *The Constitution Besieged: The Rise and Demise of Lochner Era Police Powers Jurisprudence* (Durham, N.C.: Duke University Press, 1993); and David M. Gold, *The Shaping of Nineteenth-Century Law: John Appleton and Responsible Individualism* (Westport, Conn.: Greenwood Press, 1990). I discuss this matter more fully in Paul Kens, *Justice Stephen J. Field: Shaping Liberty from the Gold Rush to the Gilded Age* (Lawrence: University Press of Kansas, 1997).

Although studies of the Fourteenth Amendment are too numerous to list, several recent works are especially valuable: William E. Nelson, *The Fourteenth Amendment from Political Principle to Judicial Doctrine* (Cambridge, Mass.: Harvard University Press, 1988); Earl M. Maltz, *Civil Rights, The Constitution, and Congress 1863-1869* (Lawrence: University Press of Kansas, 1990); and Michael Kent Curtis, *No State Shall Abridge: The Fourteenth Amendment and the Bill of Rights* (Durham, N.C.: Duke University Press, 1986).

The traditional view that prior to the Civil War the concept of due process guaranteed only proper judicial procedure is found in Edward S. Corwin, "The Doctrine of Due Process of Law before the Civil War, " *Harvard Law Review* 24 (1911): 366; Walton H. Hamilton, "The Path of Due Process of Law," in *The Constitution Reconsidered*, ed. Conyers Read (New York: Harper and Row, 1968, rpt. of 1938 ed.); Wallace Mendleson, "A Missing Link in the Evolution of Due Process," *Vanderbilt Law Review* 10 (1956): 125. Modern scholarship arguing that the concept of substantive due process existed prior to the Civil War is reflected in Howard Gillman, *The Constitution Besieged: The Rise and Demise of Lochner Era Police Powers Jurisprudence* (Durham, N.C.: Duke University Press, 1993), and Robert E. Riggs, "Substantive Due Process in 1791," 1990 *Wisconsin Law Review* 941-1003. Also see Edward Keynes, *Liberty, Property, and Privacy: Toward a Jurisprudence of Substantive Due Process* (University Park: Pennsylvania State University Press, 1996).

For early criticism of the *Lochner* doctrine, see Felix Frankfurter, "Hours of Labor and Realism in Constitutional Law," *Harvard Law Review* 23 (1916): 353; Ernst Freund, "Limitation of Hours of Labor and the Federal Supreme Court," *Green Bag* 17 (June 1905): 411; Roscoe Pound, "Liberty of Contract," *Yale Law Journal* 18 (1909): 454; Learned Hand, "Due Process of Law and the Eight Hour Day," *Harvard Law Review* 21 (1908): 495; Frederick Pollock, "The New York Labor Law and the Fourteenth Amendment," *Law Quarterly Review* 21 (July 1905): 213-214; Roscoe Pound, "The Need of a Sociological Jurisprudence," *Green Bag* 19 (1907) 607.

For those scholars who maintain that few laws were actually overruled during the *Lochner* Era, see Melvin I. Urofsky, "Myth and Reality: The Supreme Court and Protective Legislation in the Progressive Era," *Yearbook of the Supreme Court Historical Society* (1983); Urofsky, "State Courts and Protective Legislation during the Progressive Era: A Reevaluation," *Journal of American History* 72 (June 1985): 63-91; John E. Semonche, *Charting the Future: The Supreme Court Responds to a Changing Society, 1890-1920* (Westport, Conn.: Greenwood Press, 1978); Charles Warren, "A Bulwark to the State Police Power: The United States Supreme Court," *Columbia Law Review* 13 (1913): 667; and Warren, "The Progressiveness of the United States Supreme Court," *Columbia Law Review* 13 (1913): 294.

The idea of the Court serving as a forum of principle is found in works such as Michael J. Perry, *The Constitution, the Courts, and Human Rights* (New Haven, Conn.: Yale University Press, 1982), and Ronald Dworkin, "The Forum of Principle," *New York University Law Review* (1981): 469, 517.

Some recent works that call for constitutional limitations on the government's power to regulate economic matters are Richard A. Epstein, *Takings: Private Property and the Power of Eminent Domain* (Cambridge, Mass.: Harvard University Press, 1985); Ellen Frankel Paul, *Property Rights and Eminent Domain* (New Brunswick, N.T.: Transaction Books, 1987); Bernard H. Siegan, "Rehabilitating *Lochner*," *San Diego Law Review* 22 (1985): 453; and Siegan, *Economic Liberties and the Constitution* (Chicago: University of Chicago Press, 1980).

Because most of the cases I discuss in this book can be found using a title search on Westlaw, Lexis, or other Supreme Court data bases, I have not attempted to provide citations. Several recent cases reflecting the new approach toward constitutional limits on economic regulation may deserve special recognition, however. They are *Hodel v. Irving*, 481 U.S. 704 (1987); *First Evangelical Lutheran Church v. County of Los Angeles*, 482 U.S. 304 (1987); *Nollan v. California Coastal Commission*, 483 U.S. 825 (1987); *Lucas v. South Carolina Coastal Council*, 505 U.S. 1003 (1992); *Dolan v. City of Tigard*, 512 U.S. 374 (1994).

INDEX

{ *Lochner v. New York* }